Advance Praise

"This memoir takes us into the heady, rollicking—and ultimately terrifying—sixties. We are right with her as she tries to find herself through sewing and sex and psychology. And we breathe a sigh of relief when she finally realizes what one of her high school teachers knew long before she did—that he would have her books on his shelf. With passion and compassion, Pamela takes us masterfully through this story of a lifelong writer struggling to emerge."

—**Deborah Heiligman**, author, *Charles and Emma: The Darwins' Leap of Faith*, a National Book Award Finalist

"*An Incredible Talent for Existing* is a poignant life chronicle, searingly honest, and richly written. Pamela Jane's memoir is a testament to story, how its power helped her imagine, imitate, and finally create her own unique narrative. Through the beauty in her language and the empowerment in her message, Jane has given us a book that will touch the life of every woman who has ever questioned who she is, where she is going, and what the future holds."

—**Matilda Butler**, author, *Rosie's Daughters: The "First Woman To" Generation Tells Its Story* and *Writing Alchemy: How to Write Fast and Deep*

". . . incisive, funny, and touchingly candid evidence of the power of the stories we tell ourselves."

—**Howard Rheingold**, author, *The Virtual Community* and *Net Smart*

"*An Incredible Talent for Existing* is harrowing story that invites the reader to experience the thrill and danger of the Sixties from a place of safety and acceptance. It's the story of hundreds of thousands of women; our lives were huge experiments."

—**Tristine Rainer**, Director, Center for Autobiographic Studies, author, *The New Diary* and *Your Life as Story*

"Her prose reads like poetry and her imagination is like magic!"

—**Jacopo della Quercia**, author, *The Great Abraham Lincoln Pocket Watch Conspiracy* and *License to Quill*

An Incredible Talent
for Existing

A Writer's Story

Pamela Jane

Open Books Press
Bloomington, IN

Copyright © 2016 Pamela Jane

All rights reserved. No part of this book may be reproduced or transmitted in any form or by any means, electronic or mechanical, including photocopying, recording, or by any information storage and retrieval system, without permission in writing from the publisher.

While all the stories in this book are true, some names and identifying details have been changed to protect the privacy of the people involved.

Published by Open Books Press, USA

www.OpenBooksPress.com
info@OpenBooksPress.com

An imprint of Pen & Publish, Inc.
www.PenandPublish.com
Bloomington, Indiana
(314) 827-6567

Print ISBN: 978-1-941799-21-5
eBook ISBN: 978-1-941799-22-2

Library of Congress Control Number: 2015955749

Cover design by WGOULART

Pamela Jane
pamelajane@pamelajane.com
www.pamelajane.com
Twitter: @austencats

For John

"You are the only reason I am. You are all my reasons."

—John Nash, *A Beautiful Mind* (film)

Contents

Prologue 9

Part 1: An Existential Childhood 13

Part 2: Chaos Equals Eternity 69

Part 3: Bourgeois Bullshit 113

Part 4: The Voice of Liberation 149

Part 5: Starlight 197

Part 6: Celestial Fire 219

Epilogue 237

About the Author 243

Prologue

Dearborn, Michigan 1965

In 1965, when I was eighteen, I ran away to Portland, Oregon. Running away was an act of rebellion, but also of faith. In one beautiful leap I would escape my family, my past, and the insufferable person I'd been living with for the past few years—my teenage self. This person was quite obviously screwed up. She had way too many problems. No one wanted any part of them, especially me. In Portland I could reinvent myself and leave the past behind.

My brother agreed to drive me to the airport on the condition that I stop to say goodbye to my parents. So on a gray November morning, I found myself driving down the flat Midwestern streets where the silent, respectable houses stared impassively out of the dawn. We turned a corner, and my brother slowed down. There it was—the familiar red brick bungalow with my writing alcove overlooking the maple tree.

My brother pulled over and turned off the engine.

"Do I have to go through with this?" I asked. My heart was thudding heavily and my mouth was dry. I had called my parents only that morning to tell them I was leaving.

"You know the deal," my brother said. He grinned and tilted his Che Guevara beret rakishly over one eye. "Come on, let's go."

I followed him slowly up the front steps into the house. Inside, my parents were sitting at the kitchen table, breakfast dishes scattered around them.

Please mom, don't make a scene, I prayed. Just let me go.

When she saw me, my mother's face cracked open like the eggshell on her plate, and she started sobbing. My father watched in silence. I suspected that he was secretly relieved to be getting rid of his expensive troublesome daughter with her therapy bills and college tuition.

"Why does she have to go?" my mother cried, as though she were appealing to an invisible jury who would render a verdict on the crazy actions of her daughter.

How could I explain what I didn't understand myself, that it wasn't only what I was running away to that mattered, but what I was running from?

To my mother I said only, "My boyfriend and I want to be together, Mom." ("Boyfriend" was an overstatement; I had spent one weekend with him the summer before.)

"Can't you just get married?" my mother asked.

"We'll get married—later."

I was putting up a smooth front, but inwardly I felt guilty and callous. How could I cause my mother so much pain just when my dad was divorcing her? She may have been a disaster as a mom, but at least she had tried, and in her own inscrutable way she cared. Now I was walking out on her when she needed me most.

My mother started crying harder. "But you're going so far!"

"I'll write every week, I promise, Mom."

I'd hoped for a clean silent break. This break was anything but clean and silent; it was noisy, messy and painful. But it was, finally, over.

Almost. As I was walking out the door, my mother gave one last anguished cry. "She doesn't even have money for an emergency phone call!"

Emergency telephone calls were sacred in our household. My mother was always giving my brother and me money for them that we promptly spent, knowing she would replace it.

This time, however, I was prepared.

"Yes, I do," I said, digging into my pocket and producing the nest egg I had put aside for my future. I had exactly one dime.

Part 1

An Existential Childhood

Stamford, Connecticut, 1950

The Power of Story

Until I was four or five, I thought my mother was a witch, a composite of all the witches in my favorite fairy tales—*Snow White, Rapunzel, Hansel and Gretel*. Her wavy jet-black hair framed a face with cold eyes and a misshapen nose. There were whispers among the Italian aunts about a nose job. (If this was true, it must have gone horribly wrong; my mom's nose looked like it had been broken about six times.)

"You're getting so big! Almost four years old!" she would cackle, rubbing her hands together. At least it seemed to me she was cackling. Why else would she be so thrilled that I was growing older? She must be planning to fatten me up (to the best of her ability; I was a fairly skinny kid) to boil me for dinner. Since my mom hadn't eaten my brother yet and he was three years older, I figured I had at least a few years to go.

My brother was not afraid of getting eaten by my mother. He wasn't afraid of anything. He was busy catching bugs, chloroforming butterflies, and driving our beagle, Lolo, crazy by running around the house yelling "Yams!" while she raced after him. Eventually my parents sent Lolo to a special farm for crazy dogs—at least that's what they told us. And much later, my brother, Phil, would become an entomologist.

My brother was bossy, but as far as I could tell, he had no immediate plans to eat me. His plans all involved world domination and I was his first slave. He assigned me tasks like keeping the yellow jackets away while he retrieved his BBs from a frog he had shot.

Although I was afraid of my mother, I was simultaneously terrified that she would abandon me. If I lost sight of her for a moment in the supermarket, I would panic. I had at least three years before being boiled for supper, and I preferred not to spend them motherless. My mom might be planning to eat me, but she also took care of me when I was sick, made roast chicken and potatoes for Sunday dinner, and created magical Christmases.

So why did I think she was a witch? Her emotional distance, lack of physical affection, and somewhat frightening appearance could explain it. She also had a mean streak that appeared only when we were alone.

"You're dumb, like mommy," she would say, shaking her finger at me. "Don't try to be smart like your brother and father!"

And then there was *Hansel and Gretel*.

Sitting in the living room in front of our small black and white TV, I watched the story with fascination and a delicious thrill of horror. There, on the television screen in plain view was my mom—the original, primal witch—cackling over her scheme to devour my brother and me.

That was the power of stories. They told you what life was about and what to watch out for.

Lessons on Life

Paying attention to stories so I could figure out what they were trying to tell me was a full-time job, and I worked hard at it.

One morning my mom announced that we were going to see a movie about an iceberg that hits a boat.

"What's an iceberg?" I asked.

"It's an ice cube as big as a house," my mom replied.

I walked outside and craned my neck, gazing up at our two-story frame house.

Now *that* was a big ice cube.

As it turned out, the movie about a giant ice cube hitting a boat was a lot more interesting than it sounded. What impressed me about *Titanic* (1953) was how happy everyone was in the beginning—families and friends singing and dancing on the first night of the voyage—and how swiftly they were plunged into darkness and death.

My parents must have been into disaster movies, because the next movie they took me to was an Italian film in which hundreds of girls compete for a single factory job during the depression. As they charge up a stairway for the job interview, pushing and shoving, a crack in the stairs slowly widens into a gaping hole and the girls fall screaming to their deaths.

I'm sure my mom and dad had no idea the movies we went to made any impression on me. They took me and my brother along and plunked us down with a couple of Snickers bars so they could enjoy the film. I sat wide-eyed in the dark, while movies like *Titanic, Limelight,* and *Come Back, Little Sheba* charged through me like a gigantic black-and-white bolt of electricity—

the brilliant images, the glowing screen, the overwhelming immediacy and heartbreak of it all. Not only were the images huge, but the stories themselves were enormous—tales of human tragedy, simply told and beautiful in their nakedness.

These were my stories, and the stories of people around me. The broken comedian in *Limelight* was a magnified, brilliantly-lit projection of my dad. Of course, my dad wasn't a comedian and he wasn't broken; he was a scientist and he had just made a major discovery. But the details didn't matter. What mattered is that those larger-than-life figures up there on the screen were *us* and their stories were lessons in life. I learned that you could be dancing happily one minute and drowning in the North Atlantic the next, and a seemingly nice guy like "Daddy" in *Come Back, Little Sheba* could turn into a homicidal maniac for no apparent reason. And I recognized in the sad lady calling for her little dog, Sheba, a wistful sadness in myself for a vanished past, for lost hopes and disappointed dreams.

"*. . . I'll never forget that spring. Remember the walks we used to take by the old chapel? I was pretty then . . .*"

I was only five; what did I know of lost hopes and disappointed dreams? Yet these feelings were a part of me; they were in the air.

In the flickering world of light and shadows, I discovered what was real.

The Lyrical Long Ago

Films like *Titanic* and *Limelight* possessed their own dark poetry and romance, their impossible longings for a vanished past. But there were intimations of another vanished world in the book of nursery rhymes my parents read to me, filled with pictures of children in knickers and lace pantaloons skipping through quaint towns and rolling meadows.

Standing at my bedroom window gazing down through the leafy branches of our mulberry tree, I imagined I could glimpse this vanished world through a fold in time. I saw a boy in knickers and white stockings scrambling over our backyard fence, and a girl in lace pantaloons darting through the shadows. Or was it just a trick of the mind, the sunlight flitting through the leaves? I longed for this world of yesterday, for the romance of days gone by. Voices of the past sighed by me in the wind and whispered in the waiting fullness of the shadows.

"Don't forget us!" they seemed to say. "Remember, remember..."

If I was quiet during nap time, I could stay up late and watch *I Remember Mama*, a TV series about a Norwegian family living in San Francisco in 1910. Each episode began with Katrin, the oldest daughter, reminiscing as she leafed through the pages of the family album.

"I remember the big white house on Steiner Street, and my little sister Dagmar, and my big brother Nels, and Papa. But most of all, I remember Mama."

I loved the house on Steiner Street with the stairs leading to Katrin's attic bedroom. But what really impressed me, though I couldn't have articulated it at the time, was the knowledge that the ordinary events of family life could be shaped into a narrative.

I couldn't shape my life into a narrative yet, at least on paper. But I strived to leave mental notes to myself—a record of my own awareness as a living, observing intelligence. Crouching behind a tree clutching a pine cone, I vowed never to forget it. Of all the hundreds of pine cones in the world, this was the one that would live forever. I would make it live forever by remembering.

I will never forget you, I vowed, cupping the pine cone in my hands. *And I will never forget what's it's like to be me right now.*

When I was seven, my father accepted a position at the Detroit Institute of Cancer Research and we moved to Berkley, Michigan, a small community in suburban Detroit. Our new house had no mulberry tree or big shady backyard to gaze down on, just a small fenced-in square of lawn. I missed my upstairs room and our big backyard in Stamford. But already Stamford was long ago—that magical place where stories whispered in the trees and shadows held the secrets of the past.

Stamford, CT

Anxiety and Identity

Our new house was a modest frame "story and a half" bungalow surrounded by blocks of nearly identical houses and small, neat yards, unrelieved by the stone walls and green knolls of Stamford.

Most of the mothers in our neighborhood stayed home and kept house. Two-car families were rare so the mothers cooked and cleaned during the week, and went grocery shopping on Saturdays. This was great for us kids. We were oblivious to our mothers' inner lives, longings, or liberation. They were home where they belonged, and that was what mattered. On weekends when the weather was mild, the yards were filled with the sound of lawnmowers (the kind with blades that made a soft clattering sound) and shouts of kids playing hide-and-seek or blind man's bluff. But on school days, the mothers and small children were the sole inhabitants of a deserted land.

I loved staying home from school, sheltered in the safe, secret society of mothers. I had outgrown my terror of my own mother by now. Or maybe I was just more afraid of my second-grade teacher, who looked even more like a witch than my mom. Mrs. Greer had a wrinkled face, hooked nose, and sharp red fingernails that she clunked us over the head with when she thought we were daydreaming. And I often daydreamed because school seemed to have no relationship to me, or the things I thought about. (Arithmetic was the worst, especially the story problems about children buying candy and exchanging bewildering amounts of change. I wished they would just tell the story and forget about the change.)

Pamela Jane

At home, I could color, play with paper dolls, or just play with time, savoring the delicious luxury of an unstructured day. There was nothing you couldn't play with—even destiny. The characters in coloring books were unfinished people, waiting to be colored in by me, the powerful Color God. I turn the page and there is the colorless blank-eyed lady with high heels, a pocket book and no-color hair. "Oh my, it's the Color God!" she cries, as I wield my purple crayon. "Did you believe in me?" I thunder. "Oh, yes. I always knew you were coming. So please, please, don't color my hair purple!"

As much as I hated school, it did provide a temporary identity, a day-pass to the world of activity, camaraderie, and structure. At home, the long empty hours were shapeless and soft as my mother's flowered house dresses, but so porous that anything, including my sense of who I was and where I belonged, could slip through the eerie suburban silence.

All this slipping around was scary. It invited enormous, unanswerable questions that loomed up in the dead of night when the house was silent and the world at rest. Where did I fit in? What was real?

Sometimes, in the middle of the night, it seemed as if nothing was real, that sunlight and people and stop signs and houses were pictures painted on a curtain. Behind the curtain was a black hole—nothingness (nothingness = panic + death). We kids weren't supposed to know about the nothingness. Late at night, when we were asleep, the grownups touched up or repaired any wrinkles or tears in the curtain so that we wouldn't suspect what lay behind the seamless surface. Even my consciousness, my essential being, might be a part of the illusion.

An Incredible Talent for Existing

I lay in the dark, prickling with panic, and praying for daylight and the sounds of activity and life—my father showering in the bathroom, the radio playing in the kitchen, the warm air blowing through the registers. Even Mrs. Greer's steely fingernails digging into my scalp reassured me that I was alive and living in the world.

While I was panicking about nothingness, my brother, Phil, was confidently pursuing his dream of world domination. He purchased a square inch of land in Yukon territory for $1.00 from the sponsors of his favorite radio program, *Sergeant Preston of the Yukon*.

"One inch of land isn't worth anything," I said. "You can't even stand on it with your big toe!"

"But my inch goes all the way through the earth," my brother argued. "Then it comes out the other side and beams through space." He spread his arms out, intoxicated with wealth and power. "I'm king of the universe!"

My mom was bringing my brother and me up as Catholics, and every Sunday the three of us went off to mass while my father stayed home, reading. In truth, I longed to be Protestant, like my friends. Catholicism didn't seem cozy because we never went to church as a family. I thought that was part of the religion—Catholics just didn't go to church together.

Gradually, though, it dawned on me that my father didn't believe in God. It was terrifying to think that God might not exist, but it was even scarier for my father not to believe in Him. Fathers were supposed to believe in things whether they existed or not. That was their job, to be steady, unwavering figureheads steering their families through good times and bad, like jovial, good-natured Mr. Ray in the *Betsy-Tacy* stories I borrowed from the Berkley Library. The Rays went on picnics together, sang around the piano, and extracted cheerful lessons from the problems of life.

I longed for my parents to have a warm, cozy relationship like the parents on *Leave it to Beaver*. In Beaver's household, the closely-knit cloth of family life left no openings for scary existential questions or black holes, and Wally never stayed awake at night worrying about reality or the existence of God. But my parents refused to step into their proper parental roles. Sometimes they had fights (and theirs didn't end with a cozy chuckle before turning out the bedside lamp). Instead of offering wholesome homilies about life, like Mr. Cleaver, my dad spent his leisure time sitting on the love seat, brooding. This was clearly not right. And there was no excuse either! He had an ideal model of the perfect dad on *Leave it to Beaver* or in my friend Linda's dad, a high school football coach and an all-around good guy who never brooded or thought about stuff.

Once, after an especially bitter fight, my dad stormed out the front door, shouting over his shoulder, "Excuse me for living!" Then he got in our car and drove off.

I don't remember how my parents resolved their fight that day, but I do remember thinking that "Excuse me for living" definitely didn't sound like something Ward Cleaver would say to June.

Hanging in a frame above my piano is an old black and white photograph of my father, a handsome, idealistic-looking young scientist, surrounded by test tubes and lab equipment. The picture was taken in 1947, the year I was born. It was also the year he discovered Polymyxin, an antibiotic currently marketed as Neosporin. He was working for American Cyanamid, a pharmaceutical company in Stamford at the time, and was paid only one dollar for his discovery. But I never heard him complain. I think he loved his work so much he didn't care.

This is not a book about my parents, and I'm not going to probe their past for clues to their inner lives, though it's clear now that my dad was passionate about his work, and that he felt trapped living in suburbia with a wife and two kids. Left to themselves, I understood even then, there was no way my parents were going to morph into Ward and June Cleaver. It was up to me to fix this and a lot of other things entirely on my own.

*My father in **1947**, the year he discovered Polymyxin.*

An Incredible Talent for Existing

Unlike me, my brother excelled in science and math. He spent his summers catching beetles and chasing butterflies with his new butterfly net.

"He's a scientist, just like Daddy," my mother said happily.

I, on the other hand, demonstrated no special talents or even intelligence, and most of the time I felt invisible, even to myself. My main accomplishment, as I saw it, was the novelty of my own consciousness and my awareness of it. *I am here and I know that I am here* was tremendously significant, but no one, including me, saw how I was going to amaze the world by the stunning fact of my existence.

This was a terrifying thought because the only way I would know for sure that I existed (I thought I did, but just in case) was if others—lots of others—acknowledged it, which meant that I was going to have to miraculously catapult myself to fame. It was a matter of life and death, of being or not being.

In my own seven-year old way, I became a workaholic, striving to be someone—a Crayon God, a famous character in a book or TV sitcom —anything but an anonymous little girl living in an anonymous Midwestern suburb.

TV shows like *Leave it to Beaver* and *The Adventures of Ozzie and Harriet* featured ordinary kids living ordinary lives like mine.

Ricky: Mom, have you seen my shoes?
Harriet: I think they're under the TV set dear!

The Nelsons obviously had a TV camera in their living room that they switched on every Friday night for the show. Ricky probably didn't even know it was there. He was famous simply for *existing*. But I existed, too! In fact, I excelled at it, and I saw no reason why we couldn't have a TV camera in *our* living room. I would be the star in my own sitcom, beamed into millions of homes across America. I edited the film in my head so if my parents had a fight I could quickly cut to an ad. I blinked to signal that we were back on the air again.

Blink.

"Mom!" I'd call over the roar of the vacuum cleaner, "Peggy and I are going to ride our bikes over to the haunted house on Bacon Street." (Actually, the house was just run down, but we could always hope.)

"Okay, honey!"

So far, so good.

"By the way," my mother called, "can you ask Mrs. Holt if I can borrow a cup of sugar when you come back?"

"Sure, mom!"

Perfect. Kids all over America were watching to see what would happen next. Maybe we'd find a mystery at the haunted house!

Suddenly my father came charging up the basement stairs.

"Jesus X Christ! There's a leak in the basement!"

Blink fast. Cut to ad. Then start the whole show all over again.

"Mom, Peggy and I are going to ride our bikes . . ."

It was hard to get a half hour of good footage, especially when I had to keep cutting to ads.

It might be easier, I thought, to become famous as a detective, like Nancy Drew, who won the respect of her distinguished father

An Incredible Talent for Existing

and the admiration of the local police with her quick-wittedness and courage.

Peggy and I combed the neighborhood in search of a clue that would lead to a hair-raising mystery—a scrap of paper, a suspicious footprint, a rusty key. But nothing panned out. Then one night, a car slowed down on our street (there had recently been an attempted kidnapping in a neighboring town). Quickly and resourcefully, I jotted down the license plate number. Then the mysterious automobile sped away!

We waited for the next episode to unfold, but nothing happened. There was no second chapter, no subsequent clue. The entire story line collapsed.

Nancy Drew never discovered a clue that led nowhere and she never had to face having the entire plot line collapse around her. I wonder how resourceful and quick-witted she'd have been then?

Frustrated by collapsing plots and self-destructing clues, I decided to write my own story, in my head. It was all about a girl called "Pamie," and it was the longest and most famous book ever written. Most books, I noticed, left out interesting details, like blinking and going to the bathroom. My book would include *everything*. It was a serial story and I must have been churning out a thousand pages of mental manuscript a month. All over the world, people waited breathlessly for the next installment.

Stories were the ultimate reality—life rendered into perfect form with all the bugs worked out. A TV dad showing off his war medals was more real than the fact that nearby Willow Run Airport had manufactured bombers during WWII. And there was something deliciously authentic about my four friends on our block because they could have stepped from the pages of the children's books I borrowed from the library. (The fact that their names all began with "L" made them even more like fictional characters.) The small dramas of day-to-day life—Liz Ann's father coming home from the hospital, Linda's dog having puppies, a trip with Leslie to the doll hospital—were not obscure, unrecorded episodes in the life of a little girl, but events of universal interest and importance. What secret significance I found in my interior narrative, what comfort and companionship in my imaginary readers. Like a band of angels, they hovered over my shoulder, turning the pages of my ethereal tale. They assured me I would not be forgotten or erased, and helped alleviate the pain of not being entirely visible to myself.

The more ignored and invisible I felt, the richer my interior life became. Everything was alive and everything had a story to tell. Standing on the beach on vacations back East, I imagined that I alone understood the secret language of waves, as each one broke, breathing its brief tale before sinking back into oblivion with a long sigh. Others might not see any potential in me, but in my inner life I reigned supreme—author of existence, teller of tales, master of tides.

I didn't realize that by imagining myself as a character in my own novel or sitcom, or in listening to the story of the waves, I was evolving, slowly and unsteadily, into a writer. Through striving to *be*, I was becoming.

Escape to Oz

Every Christmas my father bought me a first edition *Oz* book for a few dollars from a used bookstore in downtown Detroit. I loved the musty smell of the yellowed pages, a key to a land of unimaginable excitement and adventure. I fully intended to make it to Oz myself before I became an adult.

One Christmas vacation, I was curled on the floor of my bedroom in my new red pajamas eating an apple and reading *The Emerald City of Oz* when I came to the last chapter, "How the Story of Oz came to an End." It described how the author, L. Frank Baum, had received a personal note from Dorothy:

> *You will never hear anything more about Oz, because we are now cut off forever from all the rest of the world. But Toto and I will always love you and all the other children who love us.*
> —Dorothy Gale

I stopped chewing mid-bite. I didn't move or even breathe as the enormity of what I had just read sank in. The whole universe seemed to stand still with those terrible final words, *we are now cut off forever from all the rest of the world*. I was locked out of Oz for eternity, stuck in the real world trying to coerce ordinary life into a story.

Sitting there on my bedroom floor, I went back to the book, searching for a hint or hidden clue of how to get to Oz. It just couldn't be closed *forever*.

The way Oz was cut off, Baum explained, was by making it invisible to outsiders. That was it—the chink in the wall, the crack in the door left ever so slightly ajar. Although Oz might be invisible to *most people*, if you looked really closely, you could glimpse it shimmering through the fabric of reality, a parallel universe to the ordinary world we lived in. I might not be able to enter Oz, but at least I could catch sight of it now and then.

My mother had high hopes for me to become a great ballerina, but this does not look like the face of someone destined to become a great dancer!

The End of the World as I Knew It

In spite of the fact that I hated school and my parents stubbornly refused to act like Ward and June Cleaver, I was happy in Berkley. Life was good; the summer days were long and full of sunshine and I was alive and living in a book. Sometimes it was the interior stream-of-consciousness novel—a *Proust* primer for kids, while other times it was a heartwarming story of five girls growing up together, or a spine-chilling *Nancy Drew* mystery.

Then, in 1958, when I was eleven, my mother announced that we were moving to Dearborn, an upscale suburb of Detroit. By this time we had lived in Berkley for four years, and I was looking forward to going on to junior high and high school with my friends, whose homes and yards and families had become an extension of my own.

"Why do we have to move?" I asked.

"Berkley is ugly," my mother said simply. "We're moving to a nicer town with better schools."

I was stunned. I was supposed to grow up with my friends, like in the *Betsy-Tacy* stories. Now my parents were yanking me out of my own story right in the middle of the book.

I walked slowly outside and looked around at our green corner of the world. Because Berkley wasn't the countryside I'd always dreamed of, I had learned to see a shining meadow in a small yard, a forest glade in a cluster of trees. And through imagining, I had grown to love the commonness my mother hated. Where one green yard flows into another and the long summers are yours to fill any way you want, you are free to do and imagine anything.

Pamela Jane

Now I would be leaving the labyrinth of sidewalks, playgrounds, and backyards that held the secret language of childhood. No longer would I be able to run in and out of my friends' houses, knowing as I did, that each mother was a mother to us all.

My world, as I knew it, was coming to an end.

Before we left, I walked to the schoolyard for the last time and stood alone on the empty playground. Loss, I would discover later, is a gift to a writer. Perhaps I dimly felt this, because as I stood there I sensed the roundedness of life, the closing of one chapter and the opening of another in the story I was telling myself. I would not be moving on with my friends to the next chapter of my life—one filled with boyfriends, dances and parties. Instead I would come back years later as a grownup. The playground would be deserted, I imagined, quiet except for the ghostly echo of children who had played there long ago.

The Why of It All

My new junior high school had an aura of history that appealed to my romantic sense of the past. The walk to school along a leafy footpath by the Rouge River and up through winding streets of old-fashioned houses with dormer windows peeking through the treetops gave me the sense of traveling through time, as if I'd started out in the present and ended up in the 1920s, when the three-story school was built.

At Adams, I was in the slow algebra class where everything, especially time, really did move slowly. As far as our teachers and guidance counselors were concerned, we were headed for careers at the local gas station or beauty salon anyway. But not to worry. It was okay to be dumb!

"I bet the sun and blue sky outside are just painted on the window shade," I whispered to Carol, who sat next to me in algebra. "They put it there to make us feel better."

"Yeah," she whispered back, "Really, it's dark and stormy out."

We stifled giggles at the thought of the well-meaning adults plotting to create the illusion of a bright cheery world so we wouldn't feel depressed about being dumb.

I spent my time in class writing poems and "Regency" romances that I read serially to my friend Julie over the telephone after school. Having an enthusiastic reader waiting impatiently for the next installment gave me a heady sense of what it would feel like to be a real writer. In the meantime, Mr. Spiceland, our algebra teacher, droned on.

I raised my hand.

"My Spiceland, *why* does $5x - 6 = 3x - 8$?"

"Just learn the rules."

"But I don't get it."

"That's why you're in this class."

There were so many mysteries, things that needed explaining. Like the mystery of the mind. *My* mind. According to Mrs. Renke, my elderly guidance counselor, I was an average student (with the exception of math). I spent a lot of time mentally walking around the inside of my mind, admiring the scenery, and it didn't look average to me. It was a beautiful, dangerous and wild country. Even math possessed its own dark beauty, if only I could hold on to the slippery equations long enough to unscramble their hidden meanings. But why didn't all this beauty and brilliance translate into good grades? Was I a genius? Retarded? From another planet?

And then, as if I wasn't confused enough already, I fell in love.

Don Maybee was a ninth grader who played the trombone in the marching band where I played the flute. I fell in love with him so deeply and noisily—describing to my friends my ecstasy in accidentally passing him in the hallway, or agony at just missing him—that soon half of the girls in seventh grade were in love with Don Maybee. Everyone wanted that level of drama in their lives. But Don never showed the slightest sign of interest in me or any other girl that year (in spite of the fact that I tinted my hair red and wore layers of makeup so I'd look feminine in the itchy wool marching band uniform). How could he possibly resist me? But his face was a mask, distant, inscrutable. Even his name was a riddle. Maybe yes. Maybe no. Maybe maybe. Maybe he would call in the middle of the night and ask me to run away with him. Maybe our band would go to music camp and there wouldn't be enough beds for everyone. "Gee, I'm sorry, but I'm afraid we're short on beds," our affable bandleader, Mr. Pearson, would say. "Pam, you'll have to double up with Don Maybee." Don would struggle (futilely) to stay on his side of the bed and keep his pent-up passion from breaking through.

On the last day of school, I rescued a dog-eared blue binder Don had thrown away in the band room. Oh my God. Here was something he'd actually touched! I hurried home, hugging the binder, delirious with anticipation. But when I opened the frayed covers, I found only ruler drawings of battleships, a disheartening labyrinth of straight lines and rigid angles. Not a fragment of a love note or even a few hastily scribbled words hinting at his tormented inner life and secret passions.

Obviously Don was really good at hiding his feelings.

Mysteries of the Mind

When I was in ninth grade, my mother had a nervous breakdown. I remember her pacing in circles around and around the living room as if pursued by invisible shadows, gazing off into space, her once fluffy pink bedroom slippers matted, and her pink velour bathrobe hanging loosely on her spare frame. (She loved pink, as if it could give her a soft feminine glow she felt she lacked.)

One day she stopped pacing and looked directly at me for the first time in weeks. By now my 5' 5" mother weighed 95 pounds. She was vanishing before our eyes like a bar of Ivory soap, and no one was talking about it. I was terrified of what was happening to her, and what would happen to me and my family if she didn't come back to us, the living.

She must have seen the worried look on my face that day, because she put her arm around me.

"Don't worry," she said. "Everything is going to be all right."

Her words gave me a sinking feeling. By acknowledging that something was wrong, she gave visceral reality to the fact that everything was *not* going to be all right.

My mother wore a path in the carpet, pacing and wringing hands that grew so thin her wedding band slipped off and was lost. And then one May afternoon when our plum tree was in flower, I came home from school and found the house empty. The telephone rang and I picked it up. It was my father.

"I took your mom to the hospital." He sounded tense.

I caught my breath. "What happened?"

My father paused. "She cut the television cord. She said the television was trying to hypnotize her."

She thought the TV was trying to hypnotize her? What did *that* mean? Was she crazy? I felt scared and sad—scared about what was wrong with my mom—sad about the empty house. But I also felt relieved, because no one could pretend anymore that nothing was wrong, or try to make the problem of my vanishing mother vanish itself.

I missed my mom. With my father in charge, life tilted at odd angles like a table with a broken leg. Dinners were cold, tempers short, and the unfolded laundry twisted into strange shapes. My mother might not be June Cleaver, but there was comfort in her presence and reassurance in the sense of order she created. The silver spoons she kept in my grandmother's cream pitcher, the rhythmic sound of her chopper in the wooden bowl, the white sheets blowing on the clothesline, were points of reference, visible symbols of an ordered life. Now she had her own points of reference in a private country all her own.

My brother and I were not allowed to visit my mom during the three weeks she spent in the psychiatric ward of Henry Ford Hospital. She disappeared when so much was mysterious and unknown—which crowd to hang out with, how to kiss, who to be. Her disappearance from our lives was an even deeper mystery. To me, at fourteen, her breakdown appeared to come out of nowhere. I knew she was in the hospital, but where was she really, where was her mind? I looked inward at my own mind. What was it made of, how good was it? Could I trust it or would I abandon myself the way my mother had abandoned me?

An Incredible Talent for Existing

One Saturday afternoon Mr. Brown, an old family friend from Berkley, stopped by to see my parents. My father was at the lab and my brother and I were home alone.

"She's not here." I said through the screen door.

My brother nodded. "She had a nervous breakdown."

There we stood, two solitary figures, trying to explain the unexplainable to Mr. Brown, father of a quintessential well-adjusted Midwestern family—the kind I had dreamed of belonging to. I remember the emptiness of the house as my brother and I stood talking through the screen door, the admission of loneliness, of loss.

Mr. Brown was kind that day, as always. He came in and repaired the broken TV, replacing the cords my mother had cut.

It was the spring of 1962, the year the first U.S. rocket crash-landed (unmanned) on the dark side of the moon. Is that where you went when you disappeared inside yourself, I wondered, to the dark side—not of the moon but of your mind, and what was it like there?

My mother got out of the hospital, frail but composed (i.e., tranquilized) in time for my brother's high school graduation. Phil would be leaving soon, but that wasn't the only reason our family would never be the same. Essentially, my father left us then, too. Although he remained at home for several more years, he left emotionally or more likely he was already in the process of leaving when my mother retreated to a lonely planet of her own. Who can say who left first? He had his own lonely planet. But they were never a couple again and we were never a family again in the same way.

Pamela Jane

Thinking about it now, I can imagine what my mother might have been going through. The endless uniformity of postwar suburbia made you feel that the quiet streets, wall-to-wall carpets, and ticking clocks had been there since the beginning of time and would remain, unchanging into eternity. TV sitcoms, the silver screen of the fifties, reinforced this impression by rinsing everyday life in a magic solution, and washing away the national memory of war. "Everything is okay!" the sitcoms seemed to say. But now, with my parents growing further apart, and my brother and me growing up, the illusion of suburban eternity was betraying my mom. She was going to end up alone, without a family and possibly without a home—and she knew it.

My mother, shortly after she had her nervous breakdown, in 1962.

An Incredible Talent for Existing

My mother may have vanished for three weeks during her nervous breakdown, but my father, I later discovered, had never fully appeared at all. Throughout my life, he had hidden a piece of himself and his identity, a shadow side, like a ghostly aura that shows up only in photographs.

One Sunday after my mother came home from the hospital, my parents invited some friends over for a picnic under the plum tree. My best friend, Julie, and I were talking in my room and we somehow got on to the subject of our ethnic backgrounds. I knew I was Italian on my mother's side, but as we talked I realized I had no clue what my father was. I went running out to the backyard, calling, "Dad, I'm Italian on mom's side. What are you?"

There was a sudden, awkward silence. I don't remember exactly what my father said, but after the company had left, he stormed into my room.

"Don't you ever *ever* ask me that question again," he snarled. His face was flushed; a red vein throbbed in his neck. For a minute I thought he was going to hit me. What crime I had committed to unleash such furious rage?

My mother explained later that my father was a Jew. I may have been vaguely aware of this, but I had never associated it with anything sinister or shameful, and I had happy memories of visiting my grandpa, a pocket-maker from Poland, and my bright, lovable grandma in their Brooklyn apartment.

A few weeks later, when my dad was in bed with the flu, our German doctor made a house call. I noticed how angry and agitated my father appeared when the tall imposing doctor leaned over the bed, black bag in hand, as if Dr. Merkel was Dr. Mengele and my father a helpless victim in a Nazi death camp. He was not

Pamela Jane

only ashamed of being Jewish, I realized. He was ashamed of his shame, trapped in a web of ambivalence and ambiguity. Being Jewish. Not being Jewish. Hating Germans. Hating himself for hiding.

For me, though, as a young girl, the problem wasn't so much my father's hidden Jewish identity but his not being fully present as a dad—at least not like the ones on TV.

As for my mom, she lived by her own symbols and her own mysterious logic. Years later when I was in the hospital with a broken back, she concluded I was manic-depressive because some days I wrote to her on pink stationery, and others on blue. In her mind, the different colors of stationery signaled a serious mood disorder, not a box of pretty-colored paper.

The Time Between

That spring, while my mother was in the hospital, I discovered the blues. I spent a lot of time in my room playing my secondhand Gibson guitar, picking up riffs from Leadbelly, Blind Lemon Jefferson, and Mississippi John Hurt.

In science class at school we were studying the rotation of the earth on its axis. Perched on top of his desk in the chem lab, surrounded by Bunsen burners and glass test tubes, our teacher, Mr. Kresley, expounded on how there was no space, not even a tiny chink, between day and night, just a continuous folding over of light into darkness like egg whites folded into a cake batter. My friend Julie argued with him. She was obsessed with the idea that there had to be a sliver of time separating day and night, darkness from light.

Summer came. Junior high was behind us and high school lay ahead. Julie and I sat on her porch after dinner, discussing our secret crushes and summer plans while shadows grew long and swallows streaked across the sky. It was that magical hour of twilight, a time of possibilities and transformation when anything, even the impossible, is only a summer's breath away.

Living the Blues

That summer I stopped believing in God—at least in the Catholic God of my youth. He was so cranky and, well, *judgmental*. He also had a sadistic streak, giving people the capacity for sexual passion and then trying to trip them up so he could torture them forever in hell. This sounded like the product of a twisted mind, and I couldn't believe it was God's. I needed to resolve this, because I had met a high school boy at Crystal Pool, a local outdoor swimming pool where my friends and I baked on the hot concrete in our two-piece bathing suits (no towels allowed), dived off the tower, and flirted with boys.

Danny was handsome, sweet, and funny. Usually boys went for my more sophisticated friend Mary Beth. But by some unbelievable stroke of luck, the adorable Danny liked *me*. He said I looked like Hayley Mills, who was starring in *Parent Trap*. Other than being slim and having a short hair cut, I didn't look remotely like Hayley Mills, but who cared? We walked home from the pool holding hands, and sat on the back patio on summer nights, kissing. Sometimes I let him touch my breasts, but then I'd have to go to confession.

"Bless me, Father, for I have sinned."

Inwardly, I rebelled against the humiliation—shameful secrets whispered in the dark.

One night, under the shadow of the plum tree, Danny "accidentally" bumped my breasts with his elbow. The nuns hadn't said anything about elbows, and anyway my bra stayed firmly fastened.

Pamela Jane

At the end of August, my family drove my brother to Antioch College, a mecca of flannel shirts, free will, and free sex. In this expansive atmosphere, I decided to give up the struggle. To hell with sin. To hell with hell. Suddenly life seemed very short, like the yolk of a fried egg with no white. No heaven or hell, no limitless eternity. Just the small inner nucleus. Just this.

I couldn't wait to get back to Danny, but by the time I got home, he had started going with Mary Beth. She was Presbyterian and had no scruples about undoing her bra.

In the fall, sequestered in my room listening to the blues, I began to drift away from my junior high school friends and the things that had been important to me—flirtations with boys and summer swim meets with Mary Beth, sharing a sense of childhood wonder at the beauty of a lamplight glowing through the mist with Julie. As a little girl, I had wanted normality and an idyllic family life. Now everything was changing, including me. Instead of a perfect old-fashioned family, I longed for the gutsy world of the blues filled with authenticity, anguish, and risk—for a real life fully and deeply lived, far from school, my troubled parents and the deceptively sedate streets of Dearborn.

I was the girl who had wanted to grow up and go on to high school with my childhood friends, to preserve the continuity of the past. Now I was breaking with it, irrevocably. But it was 1962; I was fifteen and in a hurry. I wanted to get out into the world, make love under the stars, be a writer. (I already had a box full of poems and short stories and had won a Haiku poetry contest on WBAI radio.)

Out in the real world, things were *happening*. In the south, Freedom Riders were getting their heads bashed in by lead pipes and baseball bats. Many of them were college kids from suburbs like mine. Even the Rice-a-Roni ads on TV, which featured a San Francisco cable car ringing merrily up a hill, filled me with melancholy and an aching sense of life passing me by. Like the hip-beat character, Michael Fitzgerald, in *Peggy Sue Got Married*, I wanted to shout, "I can't wait to get out of here. I'm gonna write. I'm gonna check out of this bourgeois motel. Push myself away from the dinner table and say, 'No More Jell-O for me, Mom.'"

I made desperate late-night telephone calls to my brother at Antioch. With his Latin looks, Che Guevara beret and confident swagger, he was a romantic figure I looked up to (though still the bossy older brother). He boasted that he'd been black-listed by the government for participating in a protest against U.S. aggression in Cuba. How cool was that?

But I wasn't thinking about U.S. aggression in Cuba when I made those late-night calls.

"Phil, you have to come home. Mom's going crazy!"

"She's already crazy."

"But this is serious. Listen!" I held the telephone up to the heating vent in my room. From the downstairs rec room came the sound of my mother sobbing, punctuated by my father's angry voice.

"Can you hear them?" I whispered. "I think Dad's having an affair!"

Lately, my father's face had a flushed look I'd never noticed before. That was what made me suspect he was having an affair, as well as my mother's hysterical sobbing.

"It's a free world, or it will be," my brother answered cryptically. He didn't seem to be cluing into the crisis at home. Instead, he droned on about Karl Marx and a coming revolution. I didn't have the slightest idea what he was talking about, but I was ready to take up arms against suburban monotony, especially if it would get me out of Dearborn.

In the meantime, I fell madly in love with my guitar teacher. Studious and bespectacled, Marc (who was twenty-one to my fifteen) was the sexiest guy I'd ever known, especially when he played the blues. If only he would caress me the way he caressed his guitar! But instead he treated me like a little girl.

I cursed my youth and virginity, qualities I felt kept Marc from taking me seriously. I was determined for him to see me as a glamorous and accomplished woman. One day, during a lesson on double thumbing, I casually pushed up the sleeve of my turtleneck to expose "tracks" I'd colored on my arm with a red ball point pen. One look and Marc would realize I was not a girl but a sophisticated woman—a junkie tragically trapped in the down-and-out world of the blues. But Marc didn't even notice my "tracks" which smeared and looked ridiculous.

In my junior year, when I turned sixteen, I got a weekend job at the Retort, a basement folk and blues café in Detroit. The Retort was a delicious descent into the bohemian underworld, light years away from my white middle-class high school, home, and my parents.

At the Retort, I found, not love, but lust with Saul, the kitchen assistant. Saul was a tall kid about my age with round glasses, lanky brown hair and an infectious smile. Whenever the cook turned his back, Saul and I ducked into the tiny kitchen lavatory and kissed energetically, his penis bulging under his lox-stained apron. Afterward, I'd hurry out to the dim smoky café to serve baklava and espresso to crowds waiting to hear Buffy Sainte-Marie or Jose Feliciano. When the set was over, I would perch on one of the small tipsy tables, legs crossed, and smoke a cigarette, trying not to cough. If only Marc could see me now!

Back home, in high school, I found new friends who seemed richer and more complex or maybe, like me, more troubled. One was Debbie, a senior whose offhanded air of confidence and worldliness belied her wide, startled-looking blue eyes and waiflike appearance. We met in the high school hallway when I lent her my waitress apron after arranging through a friend for her to fill in for me at the Retort.

Debbie had high cheekbones, wispy brown hair, and a haughty way of stating an opinion that irritated teachers, who saw her as an insufferable know-it-all.

The year I was working at the Retort, the celebrated blind blues musician, Reverend Gary Davis, came to play. Debbie and I visited him and his wife, Annie, in a run-down hotel room over the café. We were giddy with excitement and a heady sense of triumph at finding ourselves in the same room with a great blues legend, though surprised by the seedy hotel. We assumed anyone as famous as Reverend Gary Davis must be rich.

Sitting on the sagging double bed, the Reverend taught us to play his famous song, "Candy Man."

"This song came out in nineteen-five, way back yonder," he began. "I was nothing but a boy."

Pamela Jane

We watched, enthralled, as the Reverend demonstrated his picking technique with strong, calloused fingers. The muscular rhythm of his guitar and his vibrant voice erased the image of the seedy hotel room.

Exhilarated by our brush with a famous blues musician, Debbie, who was a year ahead of me in school, decided to skip her high school graduation that evening. Middle-class rituals were all bullshit anyway.

Debbie left the hotel and ran across the street to a pay phone to let her mom know she wouldn't be showing up for the ceremony. A few minutes later she came back, looking deflated. Her mother, who happened to be head of the English Department at our high school, was slow to grasp the meaninglessness of middle class rituals. She ordered Debbie to get in a cab and come home immediately.

I didn't have to leave yet, so I stood at the grimy hotel window and waved while Debbie sped off, away from an afternoon of liberation and adventure.

The Mystery of Me

Still a young girl
I have time to think
With closed fingers and no clock
Unnoticed I go—

High school poem

It was hard to imagine my father having an affair—my *dad*, who I had always run to hug when he came home from his lab, burying my face against the rough woolen sleeve of his jacket that smelled deliciously of mice and formaldehyde, a warm, comforting smell, filled with the simple goodness of his presence and the gladness of having him home. With all his volatility—he could be cold and bristling one minute, playful and endearing the next—he was my dad, and I loved him.

I brought up the subject one night, perched on the arm of the love seat where I often read him my latest poem or short story.

"You're having an affair, aren't you?" I asked, trying to sound casual and offhanded.

My dad put down the book he was reading, *Tropic of Cancer* (which I assumed was about cancer research in South America).

To my surprise, my father readily admitted that he was having an affair with his lab assistant, Pauline. He seemed willing, even eager, to talk about it.

"I can discuss my work with her," he confided.

That was understandable; my mom had only a high school diploma and, like me, a missing (or mutated) math gene.

"And we like the same music and literature," my dad went on. "Pauline even buys my shirts."

I nodded understandingly, pretending to be cool and liberated, pleased to be my father's confidant. But inside I was horrified. In a sense I could understand his wanting to escape my mom; I wanted to escape her myself. And it wasn't surprising that he wanted to join the great Sixties migration, to set out into the world and reinvent himself. But I didn't want to witness it—the sordid tale of agony and betrayal playing out between my parents.

I would have preferred to go live in the country with my mother's younger sister, my Aunt Mary, and my Uncle Rigo in New Jersey. I had spent a few weeks there one summer when I was ten, exploring the woods and fields with my cousins. To me it was the long-dreamed-of pastoral, filled with the romance of the countryside and the coziness of family life.

My aunt and uncle were the perfect parent-figures for a country idyll. They were simple, decent people. Uncle Rigo, a tall, big-boned man with a kind face and a thick Italian accent, worked as a carpenter. His greatest pleasures were tending his vegetable garden and working on the new house he was building for my aunt, laying each brick lovingly with his rough, work-worn hands. Their world held no existential angst, no brooding over Henry Miller novels, no *affairs*—just the clean solid plank of uncomplicated family life to raise yourself up on.

My parents had no immediate plans to separate; theirs was a breakup in agonizingly slow motion. But they weren't the only reason I felt trapped. Suburban life seemed to be organized in rigid patterns, like the streets of Dearborn. There was no place to put my odd-shaped thoughts or feelings, no friendly country or mind to find refuge in. This is your room; stay in it and be quiet. This is your mind; don't think anything crazy with it. This is school; shut up and study. (*That* was not likely to happen. I hated school more than ever. My guidance counselor said I was going through an adjustment period. But I was a senior now, and people had been saying that one way or another since second grade. If I waited any longer to get adjusted, school would be over.)

After urging on my part, my parents agreed to send me to a psychologist to find out why I wasn't getting better grades. I was excited about this new adventure. Maybe a psychologist could figure out the mystery of me.

Dr. Walden was a cold, prim-looking woman with a superior air. The first thing she did was give me a verbal I.Q. test.

"You find a stamped, addressed letter lying on the sidewalk," she began crisply. "What do you do with it?"

I looked at her suspiciously. Was this some kind of trick question? If I said, "Mail it," was the mailbox going to blow up?

After the test, Dr. Walden told my parents that there was no reason I wasn't on the honor roll, so the next semester I obligingly made the honor roll. When I went for therapy sessions, Dr. Walden looked smug. Her test was right.

But inside, the desperation kept building. I was a pressure cooker, getting hotter and hotter inside, ready to explode. No matter how hard I tried, I couldn't fit into myself (whoever that was). Not only that, but my family was disintegrating. How are you supposed to fit into something that is falling apart? To top it off, Antioch, the one place I thought I'd fit in perfectly, rejected me.

"I feel alone, and very, very aged," I wrote to Debbie, who was away at college.

There is no one so old and bitter as a sixteen year-old with nowhere to turn.

Reading my old letters, I can see now that I had slipped into real and deep trouble. I could find no respite from the storms at home, no escape from school, or from my own blood which felt like it was on a slow boil.

My mother had a job now at the Dearborn Press to help pay for my brother's college tuition, so the house was empty during the day. I started staying home from school, spending the long hours thinking about killing myself, writing poetry, or eating raw brownie mix and throwing up. I couldn't visualize a future for myself in the world, and no one else seemed to be able to either. I felt as if I'd fallen through the cracks. I desperately wanted to go to Radcliffe or Swarthmore, and affect an air of offhanded disdain while scoring perfect SAT scores in a casual, contemptuous manner, like Debbie. But I wasn't cool and offhanded; I was high strung, vulnerable, and easily crushed. I couldn't even smoke a cigarette without throwing up afterwards.

One day when I was home from school ramming myself into the familiar wall of desperation and panic, I decided to stop thinking about killing myself and actually do it. At the time this seemed like a reasonable solution to an impossible dilemma.

At lunchtime my friend Susan called from the telephone booth at the school office to see how I was. "I'm fine," I said. There was nothing to talk about. I'd decided to die. I didn't need to complain or dramatize, and I felt less needy than usual, independent with my decision.

Susan hung up, satisfied that I was okay. I went into the bathroom and unscrewed a bottle of aspirin. I wasn't sure how many to take. What was a lethal dose? Fifteen, thirty? I swallowed a handful and lay down, composing myself for death.

By the time my mother came home from work, my ears were ringing shrilly, which terrified me. I had imagined my suicide as a drama I would witness with grim satisfaction from across the great divide.

"Oh, how tragic!"

"If only we would have listened to her, paid more attention!"

But instead of coolly observing my own demise, I found myself very much alive, and with an alarming racket inside my head. I had an irrepressible urge to rat on myself and save this poor misguided girl who had just swallowed a handful of aspirin and now felt frightened and lost.

When I told my mom what I'd done, she took one look at my flushed face and rushed me to the emergency room to have my stomach pumped.

I don't recall a lot about that night but I do remember the two policemen who came by to make a report while I lay on a stretcher in the emergency room. They stood with their clubs dangling loosely by their sides looking young and awkward, as if they weren't sure what they were supposed to do. This wasn't a crime scene—or was it? I was unnerved by their embarrassment and confusion. I mean, if the police didn't know what they were doing, who did? As for my dad, he looked stunned and sobered for about five minutes before going back to brooding about his own life. But

I had gotten his attention, and as a result I graduated to a real psychiatrist. Cold, smug Dr. Walden, whose main achievement was determining that I could think fast if I happened to find a lost letter, had failed. I was glad to see her go.

My new doctor's name was Dr. Crystal, which he pronounced "Clystal" with an Eastern European accent. "Dr. Clystal will make things clystal clear," my brother and I joked.

I swore Susan to silence about what I'd done, but news got around anyway, which gave me a certain cachet with my friends for daring innovation. While they were filling out college applications, I was working towards my own form of higher education. Dr. Crystal was compiling a detailed profile on me. If I was crazy enough I might be able to qualify for an exclusive psychiatric program for exceptionally fucked-up kids. He talked about it like it was a really smart career move, but I had my reservations. Did I really want to make a career out of being crazy?

Nothing Is Happening

In May, after her first year at Reed College in Portland, Oregon, Debbie came home with a sugar cube soaked with LSD. We decided to split it. Debbie took her half first while I stayed straight to keep on the lookout in case she got an attack of paranoia about her parents or the police.

We walked down the sedate, shaded streets, waiting for it to kick in.

"Shit," Debbie kept saying, "nothing's happening."

That's cool, I thought, figuring that "nothing's happening" was part of the acid trip in some esoteric way I, the uninitiated, couldn't fathom. I could hardly wait for my turn.

It came the next day when I took the other half of the sugar cube downtown Detroit, where my brother's friend Bob, a tall angular black man, had recently rented an apartment.

"Shit, nothing's happening," I said, feeling cool.

But it soon became clear that something *was* happening. The walls of the apartment began to buckle and wave. Outside with Phil, the smells of urine, garbage and bus fumes loomed out of the city streets like mythological gods. Urine, the God of Stench. Garbage, the God of Putrefaction. Diesel Exhaust, the God of Nausea. It was obvious by now that my half of the sugar cube had all the acid in it, but I worried I was having a bad trip, which was uncool. To be cool you had to dig it.

I stopped in front of a glass office tower on the Wayne State University campus. Through the darkened glass, I could see office workers and stacks of papers piled on top of filing cabinets.

"I want to take off my clothes," I announced.

"No, no, that's not a good idea," my brother said.

"But I do," I insisted. What were clothes, anyway? I wondered, tugging at my green shift. Where did they end and I begin?

"Let's get out of here," Phil said, steering me away from the glass tower.

Back in the apartment, I was still determined to get my clothes off. My brother kept trying to stop me, while Bob, who had also dropped acid, sat buried in an old red armchair studying an English-Chinese dictionary.

I had managed to wiggle halfway out of my dress, when I heard my father's car pull up in the driveway. Uh oh. I had forgotten that he was coming to take me home. My brother shoved me into the bathroom and closed the door just as he walked in.

"Here she is, all ready!" Phil said cheerfully, as I emerged from the bathroom a moment later with my dress on backwards.

My father was already distrustful of my spending time downtown with my brother and his shady friends. He glanced suspiciously at Bob, who appeared to be studying the Chinese dictionary with great intensity. I noticed he was reading it upside down.

"Come on, we're going home," my father said tersely.

"No, I don't want to." As far as I was concerned, going home was the ultimate bad trip. Besides, I had some unfinished business with the clothes. I still didn't know exactly what was me and what was my clothes. I needed to investigate further.

My father glared at me. "I said we're going home."

"Yeah, yeah, she's coming," my brother said, giving me a little push.

"Wait a minute!" I said. If I could just explain to my dad that I was on acid, everything would be clear. "See," I went on, "I just took a lot of—"

My brother clapped his hand over my mouth.

"She's just tired," he said.

"I'm not tired," I said, pulling his hand away. "I'm trying to tell you that I'm st—"

A vein in my father's forehead began to throb, red and ugly. "I don't care what you're trying to tell me!" he shouted. "I'm telling you to get in the car *right now*."

"She's coming, she's coming," said my brother.

Something snapped in me. I was sick and tired of being pushed around by everyone. And who was my father to order me into the car anyway? He, who was having an affair with his lab technician.

"I'm not going home!" I yelled. "I'm *never* going home!"

I felt my father's hand slap me hard across the mouth and saw my face stretch out in a long ribbon of wailing flesh and hit the wall.

A calm anger settled within me. Coldness. Resolution. Fire. On acid, things are reduced to fundamentals. I wanted my freedom, the freedom to investigate reality, or the relationship of myself to my clothes. Whatever. My father stood in the way. He must be sacrificed. It seemed simple, logical, like a mathematical formula.

I calmly contemplated his death. I saw the knife flash, and visualized the bloody killing. I saw myself behind bars. My brother came to visit me in jail. And then, quite distinctly, I heard him say, "You blew it, Pamie."

Pamela Jane

    My brother's rebuke startled me out of my daydream. Blowing it was the ultimate uncool.
    I decided to go home with my father.

Bring Back a Story

I'm dreaming through time now, searching for the seventeen-year old girl in my past. She is elusive, but I see glimpses of her in the yellowed letter in which she wrote, "I think I can get two ounces of grass for $10.00, strong enough to blow seven peoples' minds," or in the wine-stained paper cup she caught when Bob Dylan tossed it from the stage at a concert. She is a ghost, drifting past my gaze, intent on where she is going. If I could have kept my footing, and let the craziness and rebellion be an *inner* journey of writing and exploration, I might have baffled my doom. But, as Henry James said, "our doom is never baffled."

One Saturday night when I was working at the Retort, my father stopped by with his girlfriend, Pauline. Pauline was about my mother's age, short and stocky, with a cap of curly gray hair, a deep husky voice, and an ever-present cigarette stub burning between her fingers. Her deep voice gave weight to her wacky pronouncements. But she was also astute.

"You were so young and pretty," she would tell me many years later, after we had forged a friendship. "And," she added, "you looked like you would burst into tears if anyone looked at you cross-eyed."

Back in 1965, I didn't care what Pauline thought of me. She was the enemy, the home wrecker, and I ignored her that night at the Retort, looking away when I served them baklava and spiced cider. In spite of my feigned tolerance, I didn't want my father dropping by with his girlfriend. The Retort was my turf, not his.

My brother wrote from Antioch, urging me to hold the family together and keep my parents from divorcing.

But trying to keep my parents together was the furthest thing from my mind.

"Phil, I haven't even been away from home yet," I wrote back. "I'm not interested in all this parent shit."

This blithe offhanded attitude is belied by my dreams now, fifty years later, in which I plead with my parents not to sell the house, to let me take shelter there a little longer.

If I could talk to my teenage self, just for a moment, I'd take her by the shoulders and whisper, "Wake up! This is just a moment in time. Go deep and find the beauty in it. Look into the faces around you; commit them to memory. Remember the warm air blowing through the vent where you curl up on winter mornings, the smooth weave of your black tights, the sound of locker doors slamming in the hall at school between classes. Cherish and relish each moment, even the miserable ones, and most importantly write everything down. Then bring back a story."

One night, near the end of my senior year, my father confessed that his marriage to my mom had all been "a bad dream." I was perched on the arm of the love seat where my dad was reading. For a moment after he spoke, I just looked at him. I was thinking about the good times we'd had—berry-picking in Connecticut, vacationing on Lake Michigan, discussing literature and life on this very love seat. It couldn't *all* be a bad dream. But I had to know.

"What about me and Phil?" I held my breath, waiting for his answer.

My father shook his head without looking at me. "You're part of the dream."

Sometimes a momentous moment, a turning point, doesn't feel momentous at the time. I had no answer for my father that day. There was nothing to rebel or rail against. The moment was too big to grasp. So I simply got up, walked to my room, and sat down, staring numbly at the wall adjacent to my bed. Reality stared back with a plain, pragmatic face.

"Sweetheart," I told myself, "you're on your own."

A Tale of Two Teachers

In elementary school, back in the 1950s, we were never given writing assignments, and I never imagined there were any living authors. I pictured a cemetery filled with tombstones of my favorite writers with their last names first, like card catalogs in the library:

Baum, L. Frank 1856–1919.

Writing—the pleasure of articulating interior worlds sensed but not seen—was something I did on my own. I was in eighth grade before I got a chance to write a story for school.

My eighth-grade English teacher, Mr. Mortem, was a malevolent-looking man with a low brow and small beady eyes. We joked that he moonlighted as an axe murderer. But he was even scarier as an English teacher. He snapped girls' bras in the hallway and terrorized us with menacing-sounding exams called "evaluations," which turned out to be ordinary multiple-choice tests. For Mr. Mortem, humiliating eighth-graders was blood sport. But he was the first teacher to give us an assignment to write a short story.

I was thrilled. I was being asked—*required*—to write, as if I, myself, were a real living author.

"Remember," Mr. Mortem called as we filed out of class, "no stories from TV!"

I hardly heard him. I was too excited about getting started.

At home that night, I rolled a fresh piece of paper into my typewriter, and began a story about a mute boy living in an eighteenth-century seaport. It was a dark tale about what lies beneath the surface, and about not being heard—a feeling I knew well from growing up in a family dominated by the strong personalities of my brother and father. In the story, the boy discovers a fatal crack in the mast of a great sailing ship docked in the harbor. He tries to warn the townsfolk but they dismiss him as an idiot. In the end, he steals aboard the majestic ship before it sails, choosing to die rather than live in a world that so completely misunderstands him.

Until now all I'd written in Mr. Mortem's class were checkmarks on multiple choice tests. I imagined the look on his face when he discovered the brilliant writer hidden behind the drab anonymity of a "C" student. Sure, he was a jerk. But he was an authoritative jerk—an English teacher. I was going to blast through that jerkiness and knock his socks off with my story.

A few weeks later, Mr. Mortem returned our stories. When he came to my desk, he stopped.

"You didn't write this," he said, holding up my story. His words hit me like a fist. This was the last thing I had expected.

"Yes I did," I said. But my voice sounded very small, and Mr. Mortem looked very big and imposing looming over my desk. He also looked like he was enjoying himself.

"I don't believe you." His voice was hard, accusing. My heart hammered against my chest and a metallic taste of fear filled my mouth.

The classroom was quiet. Everyone was watching, waiting to see what would happen next. Mr. Mortem leaned over, his beady eyes boring into mine. "I'm going to keep this story so you won't try to use it again in high school."

I couldn't find the words to explain that I would never "use" a story again when there were so many new ones waiting to be written.

Mr. Mortem grudgingly gave me an "A" although he didn't believe I wrote the story about the boy no one believed. Inside, I was seething.

Just wait. Someday I'll be a real writer. Then you'll be sorry.

Four years later, on the last day of high school, my chemistry teacher stopped me in the crowded hallway. Mr. Welch was a kind man with warm gray eyes and a crooked smile. By this time many of my stories, poems, and beginnings of bad novels had appeared in the school paper, but I had just flunked chemistry class. The fact that Mr. Welch admired my brilliant father made the situation even more humiliating. Now what could I say to the sandy-haired man who looked at me with such kind eyes?

Mr. Welch smiled. "I'm not worried about your chemistry grade, Pamela," he said, "because I know that someday I'm going to have your books on my shelf."

I was stunned—1965 had not been a good year. My parents were in the middle of divorcing and selling our house, scattering our family and the things of childhood to the wind. Unlike Dylan's song, this wind had no answers blowing in it—at least not for me.

"My life is a failure, as a life," I'd written Debbie, "but as a fucked-up mess, it's a brilliant success."

Yet here was Mr. Welch telling me he was going to have my books on his shelf one day. He hadn't said he thought, or even that he hoped he would have them. He said he *knew*.

Both teachers had given me a profound gift in ways I could not then imagine.

Part 2

Chaos Equals Eternity

"Come Home with Me"

During my senior year in high school, Debbie had written me long letters from Reed filled with delicious descriptions of sexual escapades and colorful characters who could have filled the pages of a picaresque novel.

"Made out on the dorm stairs with a dark, handsome math major who looks like a Spanish bandit." And a few weeks later: "The Spanish bandit vanished mysteriously. His roommate came back after classes one day and found one side of the dorm room empty." I pictured him riding off in a black cape and mask to rob a stagecoach or a ship on the high seas.

That summer after Debbie came home from Reed, we took a bus to New York to meet some of the dashing characters she'd written about, including David, whose esoteric pronouncements and notoriously messy dorm room Debbie had described in her letters. ("The dorm cleaning lady won't even go near it.")

But the David I met that day in New York was quiet and soulful-looking with chiseled features and dark, deeply-set eyes that stared into mine from across the subway car as a group of us rattled uptown to the Cloisters. His intense, unwavering gaze sent ripples of pleasure through me. I felt myself coming to life, blessed into existence by his fascination. I was *somebody*, smart and pretty enough—and more importantly *real* enough—to attract one of the famous Reed students. No longer was I a shadowy spectator watching from the wings, but a living, breathing actor in the rollicking Western drama Debbie had painted so vividly in her letters—a participant in the myth of personal significance in which, by an intoxicating sleight of hand, a group outing for ice cream became a madcap adventure, and a weird sense of humor a highly idiosyncratic appreciation of the absurd.

Of course I wasn't thinking this as David and I sat opposite each other in the subway, eyes locked in mutual fascination. But it was working in me all the same.

Six of us spent the day at the Cloisters, a transplanted medieval monastery high on the Hudson River bluffs. Its wooded pathways and vaulted halls hung with ancient tapestries heightened the dreamlike sense of entering a time and place both new and deeply familiar, an eternal land of courtship, love, and history. David and I were surrounded by people, yet alone, engaged in an erotic dance of seduction—eyes meeting, arms brushing, fingers touching as he passed me a joint behind the shrubbery. We hardly spoke, but between us was an unstated understanding that we would sleep together. The others seemed to understand this, too, because they left us alone for much of the afternoon, and Debbie conveniently disappeared from our hotel room for a few hours that night. There David and I undressed slowly and made passionate love on one of the primly made twin beds.

Technically, I wasn't a virgin, but so far my experiences didn't remotely resemble my dream of what making love could be. But now, at last, I had the romantic adventure I had imagined in all its sweetness and abandon. I loved this boy with the dark eyes and long silences, his fingers, squared-off at the ends, the shock of shining brown hair that fell over his forehead, his slim muscular body so responsive to mine.

"Come home with me to Connecticut for the weekend," David said, brushing his hair out of his eyes in a gesture that would become endearingly familiar to me. "We'll have the house to ourselves."

We were lying in each other's arms. Far below I could hear the faint honking of taxis and the roar of traffic.

"What about your parents?" I asked.

"They're down at our shore house," said David. "And I don't have to go back to work until Monday." David had a summer job working in an airplane factory.

"You'll have to hide in the attic when my dad comes home to get the mail," he added.

So, while Debbie stayed behind in New York, David and I took the train back to Connecticut together. Sitting beside him, I watched my reflection in the window, a ghostly image with houses and trees and cars passing through. That's me, I thought, a slim girl with brown hair flowing around her shoulders. What does her future hold? I wondered, as the train picked up speed, its wheels clattering against the track.

It was raining when the train pulled into downtown New Britain that night. David had left his family's second car at the station and we drove past shabby pizza parlors and dingy storefronts standing in the shadow of the Stanley Works tool factory, where his father worked as a physician.

Pamela Jane

The Fletchers' house stood in the glow of a street lamp, tucked away in a little pocket of graciousness and respectability. It was one of those square white New England colonials built at the turn of the century, with a fireplace in the spacious front hall and an ornate oak stairway with a balcony that would be perfect, I imagined, for staging Shakespearean dramas.

It was luxurious to take a shower and slip into his parents' comfortable double bed in their room overlooking a park whose trees cast shadows on the walls. With a generous supply of pot and no fixed hours for eating or sleeping, time became fluid and dreamlike. The setting, a white-frame house rooted in Connecticut soil, was itself a vivid dream image. As a teenager, I had been disinherited, set adrift, and now I was suddenly rich again, in images and memories from childhood.

I am a young woman having a love affair but I am also four years old and living in our house in Stamford.

There was a feeling of integrity about the noble old house, a continuity that knitted me to my past, as if I were still living in the house I had loved as a child, gazing down through the leafy branches of our mulberry tree, imagining I could glimpse a lyrical "long ago" of a vanished rural past. This was *my* childhood home. The park across the street was the playground where my brother and I used to swing, while David was a companion from my past and my lover magically entwined.

Yet along with the deep sense of belonging was the awareness of myself as an intruder, an uninvited guest in someone else's home. Everything about the house bespoke tradition, stability, and restraint: the heavy doors, the dark-polished banisters, the surprisingly shabby furnishings. The miracle was that in the

An Incredible Talent for Existing

middle of this spare, stately home, in the very eye of Protestant restraint and frugality, was a boy—David—not a stranger in a hotel room, but part of me and my past and, I imagined dimly, a promise of things to come.

"David, wake up. I'm scared," I whispered.

"What's wrong?" he answered groggily.

"I feel confused. I'm not sure who—I'm not sure where I am."

I had woken up with a start, my heart pounding. I sat up in bed, struggling to get my bearings. Where was I? Who was I with? The scene seemed violently out of context, the shadows moving on the wall unfamiliar and frightening. Too much had happened too fast, and now dream and reality were colliding.

David turned on the lights and together we descended the oak stairway to the sparsely-furnished living room, where we sat on a couch with a spring poking out of it, a kind of snobbish minimalism, I imagined, an old-money prejudice against showing off. (In reality. David's parents didn't make a lot of money—his mother worked as a nurse and his dad was a factory physician. In addition, they had two younger children in prep school and David in college.)

I put my head on David's lap while he stroked my hair. He seemed so caring in his quiet way, so nurturing.

"You're here," he said over and over, until I relaxed, "with me."

Night fell, day dawned, and the green rain swept over the house with its dark wood and heavy silences, submerging us in soundless depths of passion. I hid in the attic when his father came from the shore on Sunday to check the mail. Crouched under the eaves looking out at the green oaks dripping in the rain, I was a child once again, looking down into our backyard where an edge of an old stone wall was a picture of "once upon a time" torn from a book of old country rhymes.

It was still raining when Monday came, shattering our sequestered world. David dropped me off at a tiny tobacco shop downtown to wait for the bus back to New York. I stood at the window numbly staring out at the bleak wet world, wondering if I would ever see him again, and how I could possibly live without him.

Just as the bus pulled up, David suddenly reappeared, his wet hair plastered to his forehead.

"I quit my job at the airplane factory."

"You quit?" I was stunned.

"I can't work there anymore," said David, his black eyes glinting. "They make war planes."

I didn't ask questions. One doesn't question a miracle.

Back in the dim, quiet house we made love again. And when I left, I carried with me the memory of the boy and the house and the dream of pleasure, the clean lemony smell of his shirts, the hairpins on his mother's bureau, and the tiny tobacco shop where he returned for me. They were part of something colorful and wet and magical, splashing and singing in the summer rain.

As soon as I got back to New York, David called and invited me to visit him and his family at their shore home. I was ecstatic. We only had a few weeks before David went back to Reed, and neither of us wanted to miss a single moment.

So on a brilliant summer morning, I boarded a Greyhound bus to Madison, Connecticut, a community of brown shingled beach houses with sleeping porches off upstairs rooms overlooking the blue sound and white sand. David's house had been built by his grandfather, and the Fletchers spent their summers there.

Madison seemed tranquil and untroubled after the desolation and despair of Dearborn. People actually live like this, I thought—calmly and uneventfully pursuing leisure and pleasure—swimming, sunning, playing softball on the spacious green lawns. Girls ran in and out of houses, baked on the beach in their bikinis, washed the sand off their feet in outdoor showers, and drove to town for ice cream on warm summer nights. They should have been deliriously happy, but David's family was definitely on the buttoned-up side. Dr. Fletcher, mild-mannered and soft-spoken, was deferential to his wife, a thin tight-lipped woman with dark eyes and leathery sunbaked skin who seemed chronically pissed off about something. (Probably me.) Blonde, lithe fifteen-year old Kathy was painfully shy while her younger brother, Tim, made only cryptic, condescending comments. One evening, sitting on the broad wooden porch watching a softball game in the dusk, I complained that I was chilly.

"Maybe if you put something on, you wouldn't be so cold," he said, eyeing my mini-skirt with disapproval.

Though trim and fit, everyone in David's family walked with heavy footsteps. You could hear them, *clunk, clunk, clunking* through the thin walls of the summer house.

We were sitting in David's room one afternoon, reading some of my poems, when his mom yelled from downstairs, "I won't have this going on in my house!" and banged out the screen door.

Pamela Jane

No poetry reading in the house? David and I looked at each other in disbelief. But she was right about one thing. David and I were ravenous for each other and snatched any time at all, even a few minutes, to make love when the family was out.

David, and the promise of David, was continuity—an unbroken arc from childhood to a fully lived life—unshakable husbandly devotion (like Dr. Fletcher's to his wife), tradition, and within that tradition and protected by it, the wild adventure of writing. That was the unspoken subtext of my attraction that flowed through the gracious New Britain colonial, the brown shingled beach house, the sailboats on the sound, and the memory of making love on the bedroom floor on a beach towel still warm from the sun.

Flight

"Now that you're eighteen," my father announced, "you can legally live with a man."

"Don't tell her that!" my mother cried, dropping her fork with a clatter. It was September, and we were celebrating my birthday at a local family-style restaurant.

I didn't say anything, but I wondered if my father was being ultra-liberated, or simply trying to get rid of me.

My parents had met David briefly when he'd stopped by on his way to drive back to Reed with Debbie. What no one suspected—least of all me—is that I was about to run away to Portland.

A few weeks earlier, I had moved into a dorm room at Monteith College in Detroit. Monteith, part of Wayne State University, had the reputation of being an ultra-cool college within a college.

"But no one here is cool," I complained to my brother.

"Just wait until January," Phil said. "They'll start taking off like rockets."

I didn't have much confidence in my brother's cheery prognostication. After all, people didn't just explode into coolness. If they were really cool, they should be cool right now. Furthermore, I didn't foresee a great future for myself at Wayne. My roommate, who wanted to be a mortician, was always asking me to play dead, and my father grumbled about my tuition bills as if he were divorcing me instead of my mom.

After my birthday dinner with my parents, I went back to my dorm room at Wayne, where I spent most of my time lying on my bed, feet propped up against the gray cinder block walls of my dorm, daydreaming about David and the glorious few days we had spent together during the summer. We were planning to reunite the following summer. Letters and telegrams flew back and forth between Detroit and Portland.

WE WILL BE TOGETHER SOON.
SUMMER CLOSER EVERY DAY!

But rather than getting closer, next summer seemed to be receding into the distance along with the memory of the time we had spent together at David's house in Connecticut, the green oaks in the rain, and the island of happiness we discovered that lost weekend.

Weeks passed. On the city streets, the trees were beginning to turn gold. I called David from a telephone booth outside of one of the classrooms. On the sidewalk outside, a girl and boy walked by, hand in hand.

"All I want is to be together," I said.

"Me too," said David. "And next summer is so far away." He sounded discouraged.

At the corner the girl and boy stopped to kiss. The girl had to stand on her toes and the heel of her shoe slipped off, but she didn't notice.

"I could come now," I said suddenly. Why not? There was nothing to stay for. Wayne had been a last-choice option for me, my parents were selling their house, and my dad was threatening to stop paying for therapy.

"Oh, Pamie." David let his breath out slowly. "Could you?" He sounded almost reverent. "One of my roommates just moved out of the back room with all the windows." David was living in an off-campus house with four other roommates. "We can stay there," he said. "I'll dig up a mattress to put on the floor."

An Incredible Talent for Existing

The mattress decided it. I would catapult myself right over the heartbreak of the last few years and into the enchanted, mad-cap world of Reed. All that and David, too.

I calculated that it would take three weeks to scrape together exactly enough for a one-way plane ticket to Portland. In the meantime, I gave away my wooden writing desk with the spindly legs, and stuffed a suitcase with my clothes and books. I planned to carry on the new typewriter my parents gave me for my birthday, and a Lucky Charms cereal carton stuffed with poems, stories and diaries going back to second grade.

Only a small coterie of people—David, my brother, and Debbie—were complicit in my plans. I also told my psychiatrist who urged me to stay at Wayne and apply to that special psychiatric program for super-screwed-up kids. During a therapy session in his snug book-lined study, Dr. Crystal, an Eastern-European Jew, related a story of a "friend" who survived the death camps. He talked about maintaining a sense of autonomy, integrity and self-worth. I'm sure he was trying to tell me something—to give me a wisdom transfusion. But it didn't take. Detroit for me was nothing but a dustbin of disappointments—a giant dead-end. Portland, on the other hand, glimmered with the promise of romance, freedom, and fun. All the things I had missed out on in high school.

By the time I was ready to leave, my parents were preparing to move into separate apartments. My brother, who was visiting from Antioch, agreed to drive me to the airport on the condition that I stop and say goodbye to them.

"Can't I just call them when I get to Portland?" I asked. I knew what I was about to do would break my mother's already broken heart and I didn't want to stick around to survey the damage.

"I'm helping you but you have to pay your dues," said Phil, who was loyal and family-oriented but super-bossy at the same time. Kind of like a mafia don.

Later that day, my brother took me to the airport, waving from the runway as I boarded the plane. As it circled into the air and headed west, I watched him grow smaller and smaller and finally disappear.

Five hours later I got my first glimpse of the mythological land where lights waved over the dark hills and the wild green earth raced right up to the sea.

Chaos Equals Eternity

David was waiting for me at the gate in Portland, looking raggedy and unkempt in a rumpled flannel shirt, long hair, and a beard. When we kissed, his beard scratched my face, and I suddenly felt shy. This was not the clean-cut Connecticut boy I remembered, and I felt awkward in spite of the flurry of passionate letters and telegrams. I was wearing a lacy dress, one I'd picked out especially for the occasion. Now it seemed too light and summery, and out of place.

David took my Lucky Charms cereal carton from me, and together we picked up my suitcase from the luggage carousel, climbed into the '53 Dodge he had borrowed from one of his roommates, and rolled off into the mist. Only then did it occur to me that I was headed to a house full of people I'd never met to live with a boy I had spent a few days with several months before.

The Restraining Arms, the "really nice" off-campus house I'd described so optimistically to my mother, turned out to be a ramshackle cottage on S.E. 29th Street, not far from the Reed campus. The front door had fallen off, and a tattered Navajo blanket hung over the doorframe, flapping in the wind.

A welcoming committee was waiting for me, including Debbie and her boyfriend. Six or seven of us sat on a mattress on the floor in David's room, the air thick with marijuana smoke. The inside jokes and joints lent an even more surreal, dreamlike quality to the new world I found myself in. Disjointed fragments of conversation floated by as I sat, tongue-tied and terrified.

"Did you see David's room before Pamie came?"

"Chaos equals eternity, man."

"Hey, dig this photo of Andrea."

"I'm so cool, I don't dig nothin'."

"Want to go to the gorge tomorrow?"

"Where Alph, the sacred river ran, through caverns measureless to man." That was David.

Someone started laughing hysterically.

"What is he talking about?"

"He's stoned on Coleridge. Pass the joint."

In the background, the Beatles were singing affectionately about people and places in the past. One day I, too, would look back with affection at Portland and the friends I made there, but at that moment I felt like hiding in the crawl space under the eaves off David's room. I had obviously arrived *in medias res*—in the middle of the story. And at that moment, it didn't feel like mine.

Finally everyone left and it was just the two of us, alone. It was late, I was stoned and only a curtain separated David's room from his roommate, Abe's.

I remembered the conversation I'd had with David from a telephone booth at Wayne when I'd decided to come to Portland.

"I'll dig up a mattress to put on the floor," he had said.

Back in Detroit, a mattress on the floor of a many-windowed room sounded like heaven. Now everything felt too close, too real—the musty-smelling mattress, the rain splattering through a missing window pane, David's scratchy beard as he leaned over to kiss me.

"I'm so glad you're here," he murmured.

An Incredible Talent for Existing

    Our love-making had a removed and unreal quality, as if I wasn't really there at all. By the time I fell asleep it was nearly 3:00. Morning, Detroit time.

    But then Detroit time didn't exist anymore.

Reed College, 1965

We strolled past dorms overlooking rolling lawns; their mullioned windows and ivy-covered walls made them look like great English homes.

The Girl with the Oval Face

By morning light, I was dazed by the wildness of Portland in contrast to the sedate Midwestern suburbs. Bright wet flowers, like tropical birds, spilled over porches, vines scurried up walls and wound around trellises, steep flights of wooden steps raced up and down, and everything was tossed by the wind and the wild green rain.

Tagging along with David to campus, I felt out of place. He was at home and self-assured as we strolled past dorms whose mullioned windows and ivy-covered walls made them look like great English homes. One of the buildings even had the same middle name as he did, as if David were a wealthy earl and Reed his ancestral estate. He had the keys to unlock its treasures—parental support, academic credentials, and self-confidence, the very things I lacked. In a single leap through the sky, everything had changed between us. Like chess figures, we had shifted positions on the board, and the new board, I was to discover, was as treacherous and slippery as the steep cliffs above the Columbia River Gorge.

In Detroit, I had been a rebel, a writer, and a brilliant underachiever—identities that helped me glimpse myself and the world I belonged to, however incompletely. But now, in Portland with no clearly defined function and no one who remembered me from the past (other than Debbie who was caught up in her own life) I felt sketchy and incomplete, as if an artist had begun to paint my portrait and stopped somewhere in the middle.

Back at the Restraining Arms, (affectionately referred to as the "Restrainer") the kitchen sink was clogged up and the bathtub overflowed with dirty dishes. The house was overflowing, too, with party crashers, hangers-on, droppers-by, and the occasional out-of-town drug dealer.

Besides the guests, David had four roommates—colorful characters I recognized from Debbie's letters. Howard had irrepressibly high spirits and wiry red hair that made him look like a cartoon character who had stuck his hand into an electrical socket. His frisks and capers gave the impression that life was a lark and Reed a summer camp, a semi-permanent holiday from our high schools and hometowns.

Ben was soulful and soft-spoken with curly black hair, and a gentle sense of humor. Like David, he was not from a wealthy family and worked part-time as a short order cook in the Reed coffee shop to earn money. He ate eggs and horsemeat for breakfast (sirloin, 39 cents a pound).

"Yum steak and eggs!" he'd say, as if he were the luckiest guy in the world.

Abe lined his room with black burlap, twirled his dark mustache, and referred to himself in the third person as "his majesty." Sam had a round, cherubic face, blond curls, and an easy-going manner. He was shy with women and didn't have a girlfriend. A fifth roommate had fled after someone pasted Batman comic books all over the dining room table.

I might have been having trouble figuring out how and where I fit in at Reed, but other people seemed to know exactly where I was headed. Shortly after I arrived in Portland, a high school friend's mother sent me a letter.

"You're a whore, headed to the gutter with sex and drugs," she wrote in an angry scrawl. "And you're going straight to hell."

The letter felt like a curse.

"Are you okay?" Sam asked shyly, noticing my red swollen eyes.

A group of us were sitting around the dining room table, blowing a joint.

Silently, I unfolded the letter and handed it to Sam, who read it, shaking his head. "I bet her daughter is doing the same thing."

It was true—all my friends were smoking pot and sleeping with their boyfriends, but back then running away to live with David was a provocative and very public act. To people like my friend's mother I was a dangerous element who needed denouncing.

Ben smiled at me. "Did you ever notice," he said, turning to David, "that Pamie's face is a perfect oval?"

Sam's words were comforting, but Ben's put a brush stroke on my half-finished canvas. *A girl with an oval face.*

I am someone; I have a name. I exist.

Over the next few weeks, I followed David around on campus, sat with others between classes in the coffee shop listening to rhythm and blues on the juke box, and engaged in constructive activities with David like dyeing our jeans forest green to match.

Though at Reed I felt as if I were on the outside looking in, there were some things we all shared, things that gradually began to make me feel a more part of the exotic new world I found myself in.

Every Sunday afternoon, Sam called his parents in Levittown, Long Island, at exactly 1:00. We could hear his cheerful voice drifting up from the telephone downstairs, while people shot up in the bathroom and passed out in the hall.

"Hi, Mom. Fine. Yeah, I got the crossword puzzle. Yeah, school's fine."

David, Abe and I stared at each other through a haze of marijuana smoke. Within each of us, in that silent space beyond memory or consciousness, were Sunday afternoons in Levittown, Long Island. Whether we grew up in Detroit, or Phoenix, or Winnetka, we all crawled from the same primordial sea of wall-to-wall carpets, shiny linoleum and tidy backyards. These were our ancestral roots, our archetypal symbols. Sam's voice carried us back.

When Sam's parents heard from a former Reed student that Sam was smoking pot, his father confronted him over the telephone one Sunday afternoon. Sam described the conversation to us later.

"Sam," his father said, "we hear you're smoking marijuana. Is this true?"

"Yes," Sam admitted.

"Sam, smoking marijuana is wrong," Mr. Rosenberg said sternly. "Please stop immediately."

"Okay, Dad," said Sam agreeably.

There were no angry words, no tense silences. It could have been an episode on *Leave it to Beaver*. Sam's dad never mentioned marijuana again and the next Sunday, at precisely one o'clock, Sam's voice came drifting up from downstairs.

"Hi Mom. Fine. Yeah, I got the crossword puzzle. . . ."

Heidi Milk

Lying in bed with David that long-ago weekend in Connecticut, I had wondered about his parents, whom I would meet later, down at the shore. The stone fireplace opposite their bed had a carved mantle. How cozy it would be, I imagined, to lie in bed on a snowy winter night and watch the embers glow. But I had a feeling David's parents never did. I had studied the hairpins on his mother's dresser and thought about this woman—her safe and ordered life, her husband, and her son—my lover. Though I had not met her yet, I felt her disapproving presence. Even the furniture, stern and unadorned, seemed to stand by in silent reproach of our excesses. And, sure enough, David's mother had not liked me when I visited their shore house. Now, in Portland, when she found out from David that I had run away to live with him, she expressed her disapproval by cutting his already meager living allowance to the bone, leaving us almost no money for food.

"Hey, Sam, can I bum twenty cents?"

"Sure, what's it for?" he said, digging obligingly into his pocket.

"Nineteen cents for a Whiz Burger," I explained, "and a penny for bubblegum, for dessert."

In the meantime, Debbie was living what appeared to be a carefree life with her rich boyfriend. I visited her one day in his apartment and found her curled up in an armchair, reading *Pride and Prejudice*. I was impressed with her wealth and leisure, though it came to an end the following year when her boyfriend flunked out.

Next door to the Restraining Arms lived an old lady called Wilhelmina Wallace. I nicknamed her Willy Wally. Willy Wally had a grown son, a dead husband, and nothing to do but look out of the window and wag her head at our comings and goings. But not even Willy Wally's spinsterish imagination could conceive of what was going on within the walls of the ramshackle cottage on S.E. 29th Street. How could she know that Portland was the wild frontier as far as sexual etiquette went, or guess that one rainy morning, after David and Ben had left for school, Andy, another student who was temporarily crashing on the living room floor, flung open the bathroom door while I was sitting on the toilet, and proudly presented his erect penis through his pajama fly.

"Get out—and don't ever do that again!" I yelled. It wasn't his penis, which was suitably impressive, that I objected to. I just didn't like being surprised in a private moment in a house that had far too few private moments to begin with.

Dreariness set in with the winter rains, and a persistent gnawing in the stomach. The gray skies, dirty dishes piled up in the tub, and drug dealers crashing on the floor were wearing me down. At times, even sex felt like drudgery. I found myself craving an ordered house, privacy and a hot meal—all the things I had turned my back on.

At dinner we dropped by Reed Commons where the dishwasher obligingly set aside half-empty plates for us. When we weren't bumming meals at Commons, getting stoned, or having sex, we were fighting. David accused me of being emotional and volatile, a stream-of-consciousness artist-type who didn't have the discipline or talent to create. I was reading the journals of

Anaïs Nin, whom David despised as "self-indulgent and quasi-intellectual." Like me.

But he was right about one thing. My typewriter was gathering dust in the corner of our room. I was going to begin writing again, I told myself, just as soon as I got my footing and figured out where I fit in at Reed—where, exactly, I fit in anywhere. Like the drug dealers, I was a fringe element—the out-of-town girlfriend.

Meanwhile, we went on fighting.

"I can't live in this chaos!" I said, pointing to dirty needles on the bathroom floor left behind by a Seattle drug dealer.

"The Restrainer is an intellectual bohemia," said David. "Even Coleridge took opium."

"This is not an intellectual bohemia," I said. "It's craziness."

"Obviously your mind isn't the kind of mind that makes fine distinctions," David retorted.

Stung, I went running to Howard, who sometimes joined me in drinking a bowl of "Heidi milk," a comfort food we concocted of warmed milk, sugar and cinnamon. Like Heidi and Grandfather, we drank the sweet, frothy mixture from wooden bowls unearthed from a cupboard at the Restrainer.

I found Howard lying on his bed, reading a Marvel Comic book, a copy of Camus' *The Stranger* open beside him.

"Howard, David says my mind isn't the kind that makes fine distinctions!" I cried.

Howard looked up from his comic book. He knitted his brows, looking thoughtful.

"Pamie, I think your distinctions are just fine," he said after a moment. He sounded like he was reassuring a four-year old about a skinned knee, but he made me laugh.

In turn, I attacked David for being withdrawn and academic.

"So what? Everyone at Reed is smarter than you," David said during one of our battles. He didn't shout. David never shouted.

I remembered what my mother had said: *Don't try to be smart, like your father and brother.*

Was what David said true? I wondered. Was everyone at Reed smarter than I was? In the Reed library, I picked up a term paper and read it surreptitiously, the way Debbie checked bra sizes in the dorm laundry room because she worried that her breasts were too small. As far as I could tell, the term paper was not the product of a size 38-D intellect. I suspected I could write something as good or better. But for some reason I wasn't doing it. Looking back, I can see that I was off-center, not fully seated in my own story—a character out of context. A writer needs more than a room of her own. She needs a sense of being present in her own life.

But there were good times that winter too, times that resembled the Reed I had anticipated before my arrival. Often a group of us piled into Sam's old Buick and explored the untamed Oregon wilderness. We straddled the narrow paths above the Columbia River Gorge or the ragged cliffs that rose above the thundering Pacific, high on LSD, freedom, and the magical dream we found ourselves in. "Isn't this great? We can do anything!" we shouted into the rain and the wind.

On acid, we could see the mighty cliffs split open and break into the raging foam, or stand at the edge of a cliff in jeans and a flannel shirt and watch a thousand years of rain fill the seas, as if we were witnessing the world at its birth.

Even cruising around Portland with Sam was high adventure. Every few hours we'd stop at the corner gas station for a quarter's worth of gas, just enough to keep on cruising. The gas station attendant looked disgusted when he had to come out in the pouring rain to squirt another twenty-five cents' worth of gas in the tank.

When I got sick of bumming meals at Commons, I found a job as a "pantry girl" at Henry Thiele's, a fancy restaurant across the river. If I got there early for the morning shift, I could enjoy a hearty breakfast of bacon, fried eggs, and toast.

Now that I was away from my family, I found myself drawn to strong, maternal women, reminiscent of the wise warm TV moms in shows I'd loved as a kid, like *The Donna Reed Show* or *I Remember Mama*. At Henry Thiele's I met a beautiful black woman called Reina.

"This is the way you slice onions, honey," Reina would say, "nice and thin. And don't forget to have a hot lunch before you leave. They're serving sirloin tips for the help today."

When I had to go into the meat cooler, Reina would stand guard because I was terrified of getting locked in.

"Stick with me sweetie, and you'll stay out of trouble," she used to say as I followed her around on our shift.

"Are you from around here?" she asked me once. We were sitting in the small employee lunch room on a coffee break.

"No, I came out from Detroit to live with my boyfriend."

Reina's eyes widened. "Oh, honey, don't give it away for free." She winked. "I mean, if milk's cheap, why buy a cow?"

We didn't talk much about our personal lives but I was glad Reina took me under her wing. I needed a wing just then, because

Pamela Jane

I couldn't help wondering, during the long quiet mornings before the lunch hour, what I was doing in Portland, promised land of love, wildness, and freedom, slicing onions in the basement of a downtown restaurant.

The Edge of Existence

Most of our Reed friends, though seemingly independent, were supported by invisible parents living industrious lives in respectable neighborhoods, like those across from the college. They sent care packages, paid tuition, and provided refuge for summer jobs. I had no such security.

My future had not looked bright back in Detroit, but now it appeared non-existent. College wasn't an option. There was the problem of money, and besides, what would I study? I couldn't think of anything I wanted to be except a writer, and as far as I was concerned, that wasn't something you went to school for.

I didn't know what other options I had, except possibly going crazy. I knew how to do that instinctively, the way I knew how to roll a perfect pie crust, because I'd watched my mother. She made going crazy look easy. But I wasn't sure it qualified as a talent, even if Dr. Crystal had thought I stood a good chance of getting accepted into that super-exclusive psychiatric program for screwed-up teens back in Detroit.

Sometimes, on my days off, I stood on the rolling green lawn at Reed with its ancient sycamores, gazing at the solid brick homes across S.E. Woodstock, feeling like a refugee looking back at the country she'd fled. Neighborhoods like those across from the campus, small pockets carved out of the wildness, were a silent and powerful reminder of home. I stood in-between, an outcast, exiled from both worlds—the world of the deliriously emancipated college crowd frolicking along the gorges and the coast with its steep precipices, and the world of parental authority and protection symbolized by those affluent Portland neighborhoods.

Pamela Jane

As I stood there, I played tricks on myself—tricks of perception, shifting images, past and present, reality and unreality, safety and danger.

Portland was a precipice, not only the edge of the continent, but the edge of existence. Like the cliffs high above the stormy Pacific, it felt dangerously slippery. There was no safety net if I lost my footing, no place to go back to, because the world across S.E. Woodstock, the world of wall-to-wall carpets, clean bathrooms and ticking clocks was insane. I knew; I'd been there.

The Bank

Although we cavalierly broke the rules of the "straight" world, we optimistically expected dispensation when we got caught. Like spoiled kids, we were happily confident that we could pull all kinds of shit and get away with it.

One day our neighborhood bank sent me a sizable bill for a bounced check. (Now that I had a job, we had acquired a checking account.) I was outraged. Why should I have to pay for a bounced check? I couldn't help what my checks did when I wasn't around. Besides, I didn't have any money to cover it. The bank knew that better than anyone. Their demand for payment was outrageous and unfair.

I sat down at the typewriter, rolled in a piece of paper and prepared to give the bank manager a piece of my mind. Then I noticed the paper I'd rolled in had something typed on it. It was from a paper David was writing on Coleridge:

In Xanadu did Kublai Khan
A stately pleasure-dome decree:
Where Alph, the sacred river ran
Through caverns measureless to man
Down to a sunless sea

Great! I'll just use this, I thought. It'll save me the bother of having to write anything. I signed my name at the bottom of the page and cheerfully sent off the letter with the satisfying feeling of a job well done. I never heard from the bank again.

A few weeks later, when the refrigerator of the Restrainer was as empty as my checking account, Abe wrote a check for ten

Pamela Jane

dollars and signed a phony name on it. I headed off happily to the corner market to buy peanut butter, chocolate cupcakes, and a year's supply of fancy dinner napkins. Predictably, the bank traced the check back to Abe and contacted him, demanding an explanation. Instead of making up a story about a stolen checkbook, Abe simply told the bank he'd met a girl who was hungry and needed food. Confounded by this logic, the bank once again beat a hasty retreat.

Loving—and Leaving—Portland

I stayed at Reed all that year and the first part of the next.

One rainy December night David and I went to a poetry reading. The poet read a poem about the Land of Orgasms. Afterwards, we walked home watching the headlights of passing cars gleaming in the puddles.

Suddenly out of the silence, David said, "I'm not sure I love you anymore."

I stopped and looked at him, not believing what I'd just heard. As I stood there, I thought of the long dreary hours at Henry Thiele's, the winter rains, the early-morning rides to work on the stuffy, over-crowded buses, the chaos of the Restrainer.

David noticed my silence and took my hand. "If I could go the Land of Orgasms with anyone, it would be you."

I took my hand back. As far as I was concerned, we were already in the Land of Orgasms. It was a cold, hungry land. It had worn down my spirit. In the meantime, my mother had moved into an apartment in Dearborn with one of the rooms decorated to look like my old bedroom. It was her dream, she'd written me, to have her daughter back. As we stood under the streetlight in the rain, I made a decision.

"David," I said, "I'm going home. I can't stay here for us, if there isn't any "us."

David's face, all angles and shadows under the streetlight, looked startled. But I thought he also looked relieved. My move to Portland, with all its responsibilities and deprivation, had been more than either of us was ready for.

And so it was decided; I would go.

Before I left, Debbie and her new boyfriend stopped to say goodbye.

"Everyone loves you here," Debbie had said, pulling me aside. "Why do you have to go?"

"You've been living in the most notoriously crazy off-campus house at Reed," added James. "Come live with us."

Abe stepped up behind me.

"We could collect a 'Pamie fund,' so you can stay," he said. "Even if you're not with David."

I paused for a minute. The idea of staying was appealing. Secretly, I'd often found myself envying the other girls their credit cards and freedom to switch boyfriends. It would be great to hang out in the Reed coffee shop like the other kids, joke around, and listen to the juke box.

But not as a drifter.

I shook my head. "No," I said, "I have to go."

I hid my tears behind my long hair the day I left Portland. Even with the rain, the chaos, and the hunger, Portland was a gentle town. Experiences, large and small, had endeared me to the place, and the people there—driving to Phoenix on spring break in Sam's old Buick with six inches of water sloshing around on the floor and a miniature mushroom farm sprouting up under the front seat, visiting the painted desert on acid (we couldn't tell exactly which was the painted part), rolling into Phoenix at dusk with the lights scattered like stardust across the desert. There were dances and parties, bright days and dull ones, and out of them grew a feeling of love for the people I'd shared them with. And once I overcame my shyness, I discovered that underneath the darkly depressed high school girl was a comedienne—silly, exuberant and unabashedly ridiculous. Our friends were wildly appreciative, but David disapproved.

"You're acting like a clown," he said.

But I had been having too much fun to stop. Besides, the spirited high jinks helped relieve the tedium of the long days at Henry Thiele's.

David borrowed Howard's car to take me to the airport—the same car he had first picked me up in. He was quiet as we merged onto Sandy Boulevard, the windshield wipers slapping in the rain. I turned to look at the lights shining on the hills across the river. Would I ever return to David, I wondered, or to this land where bright wet flowers spilled over the porches, and the wild green earth raced right up to the sea?

Reunion

Twenty-five years after I left, I would return to Reed for a reunion. Portland looked tamer to me on my return, although the canyons and gorges, the steep flights of steps and bright flowers tumbling over the porches were the same. The enclaves of order were there, too, but they seemed to blend in more with the rest. Yet superimposed over these scenes, like a color transparency, were the images of wildness and danger I had mentally recorded back in 1965.

There was a party that first night in the old Commons where David and I used to bum meals. David wasn't there though. He was living in Japan then, teaching writing to college students.

"I hope you can come," I had emailed him, adding, "I know you would have to travel further than anyone else."

"Almost," he'd answered cryptically, and I realized he was talking about Debbie's old boyfriend—the rich one—who had died mysteriously in Mexico some years before.

Debbie, who by now had moved to Portland permanently, decided we should dress up for the party in black lace dresses she'd dug out of an old clothing trunk in her grandmother's house. Mine showed way too much cleavage and made me look like an aging madam. But everyone was having too much fun to notice. And the strangest part was that although I saw myself as an outsider at Reed, twenty-five years later, most people had forgotten that I was never actually a student there.

Ben, Sam, and Howard came, and we danced late into the night to the old rhythm and blues songs. Then, through a blaze of flashing strobe lights, a woman drifted towards me. I recognized her, though I hadn't known her well at Reed. All I remembered was that her boyfriend gave her an abortion in the dorm over spring break using a medical textbook, and she hadn't died.

"I've thought about you a lot all these years!" she shouted over the music. "Of all of us, you were the one who was really *doing it!*"

I wondered if she had the right person. I hadn't been going to school. I hadn't been writing. What could she mean?

"Doing what?" I shouted back. But she had already disappeared into the maze of swaying bodies and swirling lights.

Debbie and I at the Reed College reunion in 1993.

Fantasy No. 78

My mother's apartment looked like a doll-house version of our old brick bungalow, and my bedroom like a stage set with all my old furniture (minus the writing desk I'd given away) neatly in place. The green and white striped curtains hung at the window, and my Gibson guitar stood in the corner just as it used to.

I got a job as a typist at Grace Hospital in Detroit, where Marvin Gaye's mother worked. After Portland, the urban grimness of Detroit came as a shock. It was 1967, and driving down the icy city streets, listening to Aretha belt out "R-E-S-P-E-C-T" on the radio, I felt light years away from the green hills of Portland, the carefree summer-camp atmosphere of fun and frivolity at Reed, and the fun-loving self I'd discovered there.

Although my mother and I had little in common, in her own way, she was glad I was home. She made dinners and tried to get the two of us to be a family. She had always been emotionally evasive, but something had shifted in her when she had her breakdown. Now, more than ever, she lived by her own cryptic code, her own enigmatic symbols. The towns on a road map, for example, might hold a hidden key to my brother's state of mind if he happened to be traveling. The fact that he drove through a town called Why (Arizona) was a sign he was on a secret spiritual quest.

That spring, after I left Portland, David dropped out of Reed and flew back to his parents' house in Connecticut. I never found out exactly what happened, except that he stopped going to classes, took a lot of LSD and sat on the broad lawn in front of Eliot

Hall, contemplating the nature of reality. It was his version of a breakdown, his "dark night of the soul," as he called it.

"I miss you so badly," he wrote from Reed. "I've been so careless, so wasteful of your love. Will you take me back?"

For the first time, I saw David as psychically vulnerable, which made him more loveable and endearing. The hardships of life in Portland—the rain, the hunger, the fights—began to fade. David was distraught. And I, too, was shocked at the reality of finding myself back in the Midwest, as if I had fallen asleep in Portland and awakened in Detroit, alone and with all my plans for the future shattered. Without each other, our lives felt fractured and incomplete. Once again telegrams flew back and forth.

I'M SO ALONE HERE.

WE WILL FIND A WAY TO BE TOGETHER.

We needed a permanent glue to hold us together forever—to state to the world and to ourselves that nothing would ever tear us apart again. This required a radical step, something none of our friends had dreamed of doing. We decided to put our faith in an outdated tradition, hoping it would work its ritual magic. We would get married.

At Reed, David had studied Blake and the Christian mystics. Now he talked about going to divinity school. A wave of images flooded my mind—a small New England town tucked into the hills, a gracious old rectory, children running through the yard, a rope swing tied to an apple tree. I had a huge inventory of stock fantasies from books and old movies I'd watched on late-night TV. Fantasy No. 78—minister's wife, old rectory, children, apple pies. David joked that he would take long acid trips and write short sermons. I'd give teas and write. We'd have a close, cozy family like in the *Betsy-Tacy* books I'd loved as a child.

Sitting in my recreated childhood room, I wrote a poem for David:

> *Now is the time*
> *Now is the time*
> *A minister for a husband*
> *The wafer and wine*
>
> *Now is the time*
> *Now is the time*
> *The minister's wife*
> *From God's table must dine*

To dine from God's table was to take part in all that was fruitful and fulfilling, to live in a warm, believing reality of candles, choirs, and church picnics, weaving myself securely into a busy, active life so I'd never fall out of my story into a void or a desolate night of the soul.

David's parents had been furious when I went to live with him in Portland. Now they were even more pissed off that I'd left, claiming I'd precipitated his disintegration at Reed. I flew to Connecticut to talk over marriage plans with them. I sat next to David on the tattered couch in the living room, his mother shaking with rage at the idea that her son was marrying a college drop-out from a broken family. His father, the kindly physician, offered an explanation.

"If you were from Circle Beach or went to Smith"—Dr. Fletcher smiled apologetically—"things would be different."

It was painful to sit in that room, thick with tension, and face these people who felt I wasn't good enough to marry their son. But of course I wasn't really there and this wasn't really happening. What was happening was that I, Elizabeth Bennet, the brilliant heroine of my favorite novel, *Pride and Prejudice*, was standing up to the arrogant Lady Catherine de Bourgh in the scene where she confronts Elizabeth with a rumor that she is engaged to marry Lady Catherine's wealthy and distinguished nephew, Mr. Darcy.

Lady Catherine: *"If you were sensible of your own good, you would not wish to quit the sphere, in which you have been brought up."*

"In marrying your son, I should not consider myself as quitting that sphere. He is a gentlemen; I am a gentleman's daughter; so far we are equal."

"True. You are a gentleman's daughter. But who was your mother? Who are your uncles and aunts? Do not imagine me ignorant of their condition."

My father was a scientist; David's father was a physician. So far we were equals. But who was my mother? An uneducated woman, the daughter of Italian immigrants (most of David's ancestors had come over on the Mayflower), a divorcée with a dubious mental history.

"This will be a marriage built on sugar cubes," David's father predicted darkly, shattering my *Pride and Prejudice* fantasy. He was referring to the sugar cubes laced with LSD David had hidden at the shore house when I was visiting, and which his parents had later discovered.

In response, David buried his face in his hands and wept like a girl.

A Little Voodoo (Goes a Long Way)

David's vulnerability touched me.

"We want to get married," he said over and over, while his parents looked on in stony silence.

How could I have thought he was unfeeling? How could I have been so unfeeling myself, accusing him of being a dry academic?

As a writer, you long to edit your life, to get your hands on the living manuscript. Cut this chapter out. Delete this one completely. Maybe I should have listened to David's parents and left him then and there. Maybe I should have moved to Circle Beach, or gone to Smith. Instead, David and I got married.

My father accepted David, although he called him a "hopeless scholar." My mother was pleased that her wild nineteen-year-old daughter was finally settling down.

That August, in 1967, we got married at a Presbyterian church in New Britain. David's family came up from their shore house, his brother and sister silent and shadowy as two ghosts, his mother pale and tight-lipped. They spoke to no one and left immediately after the ceremony.

My parents and my brother, Phil, came, too. Miraculously, my mother and father got along beautifully that day, as if they were still together—a lovely and unexpected wedding gift. In the evening my father took us all to a country inn for dinner.

After the wedding, we packed our few belongings and moved to an apartment on the Lower East Side of Manhattan.

"It's a lovely apartment," the realtor assured us, "and it's only seventy dollars a month!"

Pamela Jane

Our lovely apartment had a hole in the living room floor the size of the Grand Canyon and an unconscious body in the downstairs hall. The tub was in the kitchen, and when I took a bath cockroaches fell out of the cupboards, tangling themselves in my long hair. This place made the Restraining Arms look like the Ritz Carlton.

David enrolled at The New School for Social Research and I got a job working as an artist's model. The modeling agency was run by Martine, a tall exotic-looking Haitian woman, and her cousin, Jim. Martine checked out the jobs to make sure everything was on the up and up.

"Three hours at Queensborough Community College, how soon can you get there? . . . Brooklyn Museum of Art tonight . . . West 20th street tomorrow. That one's a private guy. He's all right as long as he doesn't take out the vibrator." (I turned that one down.)

I liked modeling because I could be alone with my thoughts. As the artists' charcoal scraped across the paper, I told myself stories of my life, shaping the events into a narrative, just as I had as a little girl. The story went right up to the present, to the young woman who sat naked, wrapped only in a cloak of solitude and reflection. Weaving a story from the past made me feel integrated and prepared for the next chapter of my life.

I wanted that chapter to start soon because living in New York wasn't exactly marital bliss. Junkies broke into our apartment the first day we moved in and stole the new silverware David's grandmother had given us as a wedding gift. Boom boxes and sirens screamed outside our windows. When a rat raced across our bed one night, I exploded.

An Incredible Talent for Existing

"That's it. We're getting out of here!" I yelled. "You can commute to school."

Instead of a country parsonage with children running through the dappled sunlight, I'd landed in yet another slum. But *this* time I was determined to realize my dream. We would move to the country, that magical place where stories lived and romance waited. Where I would begin to write again.

My strategy was simple. Take a train to the country and find a house to rent.

But which train, in which direction?

David and I were standing in the middle of Grand Central Station at rush hour. I opened a schedule and read the names of the stops out loud, while people pushed past us, hurrying to make their trains.

"Cos Cob, Riverside, Old Greenwich . . . Stamford! David, Look!" I cried pointing to the schedule. "There's a train to Stamford! We can move back to where I grew up!"

"We can't afford to live in Stamford," said David, peering over my shoulder. "Anyway, it's not the country."

Undaunted, I picked up another schedule.

"Here's another line that goes to Cold Spring, New York. That sounds like the country." I imagined a picturesque cottage by a bubbling spring.

"You can't tell by the name, Pamie. Anyway, we don't have a car. What are we going to do when we get there?"

David had a point. We had no money for a car or a rental security deposit. The truth is, it would take a miracle to get us out of New York. My dream of a country house looked hopeless.

So we went back to our apartment without having stepped onto a single train.

Then, in the fall of 1968, when we'd been living in New York for a year, I came across an ad in *The Village Voice*:

"Country cottage for rent ninety miles north of New York City. $100 a month including utilities."

"Oh, my God. David, this is it!"

Then I noticed the date. The ad was a month old. New York was overflowing with couples trying to escape their rat-and-roach-infested apartments on the Lower East Side and move to a country cottage, I imagined. This one must have been snapped up immediately. But I called anyway. Miraculously, the cottage was still available. It was three miles from the nearest town, so we could hitchhike in to buy groceries. And no security deposit was required. There was only one snag.

"Lots of people have called, but their energy wasn't right," the owner told me on the phone. "I could tell just by talking to them."

"How's our energy?" I asked anxiously.

"I'll have to meditate on it."

I hurried off to Martine's tall handsome cousin, Jim.

"Jim, you have to do voodoo to fix our energy."

Jim scowled. "Voodoo is serious stuff. It's nothing to mess with."

"Please? We have to get this country cottage!"

I don't know what dark rituals Jim performed, but later that night the owner called back to tell us the country cottage was ours.

Part 3

Bourgeois Bullshit

Long Ago in the Here and Now

New Paltz, New York, is an old town, built on the banks of the sleepy Wallkill River. From up on the hill near the state college, the land unfolds like a bolt of green cloth, rippling down past shops and houses to the river flats, where it flows over the fields and rises up to form the magnificent Shawangunk ridge.

Our cottage was a two-story annex to an eighteenth-century stone house. The three upstairs rooms with their wide pine floorboards and low ceilings had the sweet musty smell of a country attic in the summer. I walked down the hall to a small room with a wooden-planked door painted green like a garden gate.

"David, look. My writing room!"

Moving to the country was like opening a page to a forgotten book filled with pictures of a vanished past called Long Ago. Here, in my writing room, I would find solace in silence, and stories in the shadows that swelled beneath the apple tree below. To me, the woods and fields were more beautiful than the rain forest and wild gorges of Oregon; that was exotic beauty, while this was familiar beauty—the beauty of the past.

We walked down the road to Dietz's Dairy farm, that first afternoon, carefully carrying the tin pail filled with foamy milk on the way home. When night came, I lay in bed beside David with the green meadows spread around me in the dark. Life, as Thoreau wrote, had a wide margin, and I liked it.

I found a part-time job in town at Vick's Dry Cleaners. Early every morning I walked three miles into New Paltz, past maple trees whose glowing leaves lit the way back to the autumns of my childhood. Cows stared at me over stone fences lined with bright pumpkins and yellow squash, and the air smelled pungently of manure and fallen apples. After the Lexington Avenue subway, this was paradise.

I worked the morning shift at the cleaners, ringing up customers, tagging the clothes for cleaning, and chatting with Nellie, who did the mending.

Betty took over from me in the afternoon. She was burly and masculine with short, slicked-down hair and baggy woolen pants that made her look like a bus driver. She walked around acting as though she owned the place and quoting her father, the ultimate authority on everything.

"Dad says we're in for a rough winter," or "Dad says a John Deere snowplow is the only kind to buy."

Vick, the owner, was large, affable and easy-going. His middle-aged girlfriend, Helen, who dressed like Dolly Parton with tight blue jeans and a puffy blonde wig, ran the business and supervised the help. Sometimes I stayed after Betty took over to visit with Helen, gossiping and giggling over cups of steaming tea in the tiny apartment she shared with Vick above the shop. Our chats were punctuated by the complaints of Pepsi, a scrawny, ill-tempered Siamese cat Helen kept tied to the refrigerator because he threw up all the time.

Betty invariably interrupted these cozy tête-à-têtes, much to Helen's annoyance.

"The oil delivery man is here and there's no money to pay him with!" she would shout up the stairs triumphantly.

To Helen, Betty was the human version of Pepsi, only Helen couldn't tie her to the refrigerator.

Everything at the cleaners was rundown and falling apart in an easy, comfortable way—the cavernous old building, the rattling brown delivery truck, even the business itself. To me, the shop was a stage set where townsfolk made their entrances and exits with the jingle of the brass bell. Because it had the sense of make-believe, it took on a fuller reality for me, rounder and more supple and alive than ordinary life. All the town characters—Pete, the owner of the movie theater; Mrs. Walker, the librarian; Big Bo from the hippie boutique—each played his part and spoke his piece in turn.

David got a part-time job driving the dry cleaning delivery truck, and Vick's became a second home for both of us. In their own way, Helen, Betty and the others were as eccentric as any of our Reed friends, and David and I fit snugly into their quirky world and the college town full of anti-establishment kids like us.

Most days, when my shift was over, I was out the door, down Main Street and on to the open land in a minute, the whole glorious September afternoon shining before me.

This was the place and time—the very moment, I had been waiting for. On all my travels, crisscrossing the country, I had carried along the Lucky Charms cereal carton filled with my stories, journals, and poems. The yellowed pages held the promise of redemption from the failure and anonymity that had haunted me since I was a little girl trying to make my life into a TV sitcom watched by millions. Now I carried the box upstairs to my green-gated room, where I could see the curve of the mountains rippling through the wavy old glass.

Sitting cross-legged on the floor, I opened the bulging carton, which was beginning to fray around the edges. On top was a poem I had written in Mr. Spiceland's seventh grade algebra class:

> *In an old seaport, not known to me*
> *Ticked the strangest clock*
> *By the edge of the sea.*
> *It kept the seaport in perfect time—*
> *The sailors sailed home*
> *When they heard it strike nine . . .*

I pulled out a stack of photos of high school classmates with messages scrawled on the back: "I will always remember your talent for creative writing"; "I can't wait to read your first book!" I smiled to myself. At last, I could fulfill that promise and pick up the threads I had dropped in high school. But where to begin? I imagined myself continuing a literary tradition of greatness, writing a book that would combine the novels of George Eliot, feminist Kate Millet's *Sexual Politics*, the *Oz* books, and Aretha Franklin's soul music. It would be brilliantly perceptive, uncompromisingly feminist, yet with a naïve childlike-quality and a touch of the blues, all woven together with the beauty and warmth of a country quilt. No wonder I felt stymied!

Shifting my weight on the floor, I frowned, puzzled. What would such a piece of writing actually look like? I sighed. Then slowly, I placed the poem and high school pictures carefully back in the carton and slid it under the long table I planned to use as a desk. I would open it again tomorrow, I promised myself.

I had taken a sewing class at night school in New York. Now, instead of writing in my green-gated room, I began to sew on my second-hand Singer sewing machine, using pieces of fabric that reflected country life around me—calico prints as fine as old china, yellowed lace that glowed like lamplight, a pattern of wild flowers in summer fields.

I wasn't much of a cook, but I loved baking pies, and spent long afternoons alternately baking and sewing—roll out the dough, roll out the fabric, shape the dough, shape the dress, trim the crust, trim the cloth. Upstairs and down I went, from the sewing room to the kitchen like a needle weaving back and forth through the cloth.

David loved the pies and bell-bottom trousers I made him. He, too, was settling comfortably into rural life, even though it meant hitchhiking to New York two days a week to attend classes at The New School. We spent peaceful evenings listening to the dying song of the crickets, David reading Joyce's *Ulysses* while I curled up in a faded armchair writing long letters to Debbie, who by then had graduated from Reed and was living in San Francisco, pursuing photography and guys.

David remained skeptical about my becoming a writer. "Your writing illustrates tendencies I deplore," he said during one of our arguments. He was referring to my imitations of Anaïs Nin, whom he had special contempt for.

"Well, look at you!" I shot back. "You have no creativity, no imagination, no fire! You're just a boring academic who feeds off of other people's creations."

"That's better than being a self-indulgent, pseudo-intellectual," David retorted. "Just because a few people wrote what a great writer you are on the back of their high school pictures doesn't make you a brilliant artist."

"Well at least it shows I have promise."

"Promise!" David scoffed. "You have to *produce*. Why don't you go back to school?"

But I didn't know what I wanted to study. I also didn't know any writers, back then, who had struggled through bad drafts to publish successful books, and I had no idea that such a struggle was a part of a writer's development. I expected my inner brilliance to come out intact on the first draft. Either you were a born genius or you're weren't.

I think that David was terrified that his own gifts would go to waste and his life end unremarkably. Like Debbie, he had achieved perfect SAT scores, and was a gifted academic writer. Perhaps he also harbored a dream of becoming a great novelist—a dream he was afraid to believe in. We were bound together in mutual terror, lashing out at each other.

His mother, on the other hand, had faith in her son.

"David is going to be a great writer like F. Scott Fitzgerald," she commented on our first married Thanksgiving, which we spent at his family's house in Connecticut. I never felt welcome when we visited, but sat in the living room, hands folded, the perpetually unwanted guest.

"His wife Zelda was crazy," she went on, looking at straight at me. "She wanted to be a writer, but she never amounted to anything."

My two biggest fears—going crazy and never amounting to anything.

How did she know?

New Paltz, NY, 1968

The upstairs rooms with their wide pine floorboards and low ceilings had the sweet musty smell of a country attic in the summer.

Bourgeois Bullshit

When he wasn't going to school in New York, David continued to drive the rural delivery route for the dry cleaners. The days were growing shorter, and it was often dark by the time the rattling brown delivery truck pulled up. I often hitched into town to wait for him at the cleaners where Helen and I sat around talking about people and cats we loved and hated. If Gene, the presser, was working, the smell of warm wool would emanate from the back room while Helen made plans to fire bossy Betty or dump Pepsi off at a cat farm—promises we both knew she would never keep. Outside the wind whistled through the grass and the autumn mountains turned a colder shade of purple.

On nights he hitchhiked home from New York, David walked under the stars from the thruway exit to our house on Springtown Road. It was on one of those starry nights when the house was filled with the smell of warm apple pie and fat flies buzzed at the old windows of the sewing room that he told me he was going to jail.

"I'm going to refuse induction to protest the war," David said, his eyes blazing under the lock of hair that fell over his forehead.

It was 1968 and rallies against the Vietnam War raged across college campuses and in the streets of Washington D.C. But I was stunned by his announcement. In high school my brother and I had boarded a dilapidated school bus and ridden to Washington to protest the war. But a high-spirited teenager marching on Washington was different than a husband whose idea of a honeymoon was three years in a federal penitentiary.

Besides, our friends had never talked about politics at Reed; it was considered uncool to be too serious about anything.

"Can't we just run away to Canada?" Lots of conscientious objectors were doing that.

David's dark eyes glittered.

"Pamie! You. Don't. Understand." His words sounded hard and clipped, as though chiseled from stone. "This war is an attempt to stifle the spontaneous quest for liberty by a people oppressed for thirty years. It is—" David paused, searching for the words "—the last gasp of imperialism upon the earth."

It was the longest sentence he had ever spoken. But I wasn't thinking about the last gasp of imperialism.

"I thought you were going to finish school and be a minister! And what about having kids?"

"Having kids is self-indulgent and bourgeois. Besides, the revolution is coming."

Was he nuts? What about our future life in a white frame house in New England, and the corner lot with maple trees and college co-eds strolling by? We would be like the couple in *Who's Afraid of Virginia Woolf?* only happy. Now our future was, at least temporarily, totally fucked.

"It's all because of the Resistance," I complained to Debbie from the telephone booth outside the bus depot in town (we had no telephone at home). The Resistance was an anti-war organization David had joined at The New School.

"They don't even believe in the personal freak-out!" I added. I was a devout practitioner of the personal freak-out. Even in the idyllic rural setting of New Paltz, I was often assaulted by free-floating anxiety that could be crippling. Sometimes it seemed I was just freaked out about existence; I am, therefore I panic.

"Yeah, all that personal angst is bourgeois bullshit." I could hear Debbie exhaling her unfiltered Camel on the other end of the line. She too had a boyfriend who considered himself a revolutionary.

David was into facing contradictions, as in the "contradictions of capitalism" or "class contradictions." It was a contradiction to be a revolutionary and not wage war.

"There's no such thing as a passive radical. You're either making bombs or you're not."

It was like being a writer. Either you were Shakespeare, or you were shit.

I was into contradictions, too—the contradiction of why I desperately missed Portland although life there had been hard, the contradiction of why I'd moved to the country to write but I couldn't get started, the contradiction of how I'd escaped the ghetto of the Lower East Side only to find myself a prisoner of my husband's ideology. In David's view, it was anti-revolutionary to have kids, bourgeois to own a car, and fascist execution to kill an insect. That last taboo I discovered one day when I spotted an unwelcome visitor in the bathtub.

"David!" I screamed. "There's a giant cockroach in the tub!"

"Giant" wasn't the word for it. This was the Godzilla of roaches. David hurried into the bathroom.

"That's only a water bug," he said, peering over my shoulder. "It probably crawled up from the drain."

Pamela Jane

"*From the drain?*" I was horrified. There could be more giants lurking down there. "I'm getting the Drano," I said, heading to the kitchen.

"You're going to *kill* it?"

"No, just discourage it a little," I mumbled, rummaging under the kitchen sink. I came back carrying the can of Drano.

David glared at me. "You know that Drano liquefies organic matter."

"Well, at least it won't come back." I turned the water on full-force and unscrewed the Drano cap.

"Why don't you just call in the National Guard?" David said bitterly, and stalked out of the bathroom slamming the door.

Before we had gotten married we visited a minister for the required pre-marital counseling.

"I presume you are sexually compatible?" he had asked.

David and I exchanged glances. "Sure," he said, hiding a smile.

I nodded. "Absolutely."

The minister should have isolated us in separate rooms and interrogated us about our hopes, our dreams, our ambitions. Then, if one of us had said, "I long to live in an old country parsonage, bake pies, have children, and write," while the other had confessed he wanted to die fighting a guerilla war in the Catskills, he could have offered some gentle counseling to smooth out small incompatibilities.

In spite of our differences, David and I were happy together that fall. We took long walks along the ridge of the mountain overlooking the flaming Wallkill river valley, scrambled over rocky crags, and spent quiet evenings reading. Nights were filled with love-making while the crickets chirped sleepily outside our window.

I filled cracked ceramic vases with Japanese Lanterns and placed them on the deep window sills. But like the vases, our peaceful pastoral life had a web of fine cracks running through it. And the cracks were growing wider.

New Paltz, NY

"The land unfolds like a bolt of green cloth where it flows over the fields and rises up to form the magnificent Shawangunk ridge."

The Greatness of the Unwritten Novel

I was reading *Middlemarch*, by George Eliot, when I came across this passage:

> *"Many Theresas have been born who found for themselves no epic life . . . perhaps only a life of mistakes, the offspring of a certain spiritual grandeur ill-matched with the meanness of opportunity; perhaps a tragic failure which found no sacred poet and sank unwept into oblivion."*

These words sent shock waves through me. With every step I took, past gold-rimmed mountains and autumn cornfields, I felt myself sinking "unwept into oblivion." I was surrounded by ineffable beauty but I had no framework or organizing principle to help shape it. To give myself a sense of significance and purpose, I began to imagine myself as Dorothea, *Middlemarch*'s idealistic, passionate heroine. I too, was "the offspring of a certain spiritual grandeur ill-matched with the meanness of opportunity." And it was less painful to see myself as the heroine of a great novel than to face the fact that my life was going nowhere. A heroine in a novel may go nowhere, but she goes nowhere eloquently, with significance, pathos, and high visibility. Moreover, she is not alone; she is supported by the invisible web of the novel, part of a divine plan not detectable to ordinary mortals.

Everything that was wrong in my life—the fights with David, failures and frustrations, the fact that I wasn't writing—I saw as elements of the story I was living. Ordinary moments of being were translated, with mental lightning, into brilliant prose. Once again, as when I was a child, I was writing imaginary novels in my head.

The sadness and sense of loss for a vanished age that permeate Eliot's *Middlemarch* and *Mill on the Floss* lent New Paltz a deeper dimension. I visualized myself, pen in hand, sketching for my imaginary reader the river town with its façade of modern buildings, through which you could glimpse the village of the 1930s, the 1800s, all the way back to the original seventeenth-century settlement of stone houses scattered along the river. This sense of creating a rich historical setting knitted me deeply to the town and the land around it, as if *my* ancestors had farmed the rich river flats and built the old lumber mill by the river.

In my sewing room, all my unarticulated ambitions flowed into the cloth that I cut and stitched into a shapely whole. The long flowered dresses I made were characters who could have stepped from the fairy tales I loved as a child—the woodcutter's daughter, the princess, the peasant girl. The old tales flowed through my dreams, as the cloth, warm from the iron, flowed under my fingers.

Anything I could imagine, I could sew, and I was a chain sewer. As soon as I put the finishing touches on one garment, I unrolled the fabric for the next one. And though I sometimes wore a comfortable calico dress to the dry cleaners, most of the dresses I made, such as the Regency gown fashioned from old silk curtains, hung like ghosts in my closet.

To add richness and depth to my eloquent silence, I began to gather things around me from yard sales and thrift shops—baskets, rag rugs, and old quilts. These things, shaped by the hands of unseen women in a forgotten past, were indescribably beautiful to me—the untold stories of all the Dorotheas.

The winds whistling through the dry grass sang of winter to come. In my warm, lighted upstairs room, I sat sewing and listening to the silence. There was no telephone, no TV or radio, nothing to distract me. Next door, the old stone house slept and in its sleep I sensed spirits moving quietly from room to room like shadowy elements of an unformed story. Slowly, they began knitting together the fragments of the past, piecing them into an articulate whole. But this was no more than a dim sense of movement beneath the surface of country solitude, an intimation of things to come.

"The old tales flowed through my dreams, as the cloth, warm from the iron, flowed under my fingers."

Eddie

Two years had passed since we moved to New Paltz. David had refused induction; his trial was scheduled to take place in New Haven. In the meantime, he quietly stopped going to classes at The New School. Maybe he was influenced by my anti-academic attitude. Fellow radicals extolled this as a virtue since they viewed academia—the "history of dead white men"—as irrelevant and reactionary. But the truth was, I just couldn't figure out what to study. In any case, David dropped out of school. He was just a dry cleaning deliveryman now, and I was a counter clerk.

Well, not exactly. For I was a radical now, too. Women's liberation had ignited my rage against men, the "system," academia, the nuclear family and everything else I imagined had screwed up my life. In my women's consciousness-raising group, which was composed of students and newlyweds like myself who met at the back of the health food store, we talked about how to rewire men biologically so they wouldn't be pigs. Love between a man and a woman was all bourgeois bullshit anyway. I stopped shaving my legs and threw away my bras.

And then, right in the middle of my most militant man-hating phase, I fell in love with Eddie.

David and I had a bigger fight than usual that December day. (Or maybe, looking back, it just seems bigger because it opened a crack that everything, including Eddie, fell into.) David was furious because he thought I was looking forward to his going to jail.

"You can't wait!" he said accusingly.

"Well, it wasn't my idea!" I retorted. But inwardly I knew he was right. With all our conflicts—about my writing, politics, and what kind of life we could possibly build together—jail for him was starting to look more and more like liberation for me.

To defuse our sore feelings, David and I hiked over the mountain to an old hunter's cabin where Eddie lived with his girlfriend, Mira. Both of them were students at the state college, living marginal lives like ours, with no luxuries and little money to spare. The four of us had spent many winter evenings at their cabin, roasting potatoes in the glowing coals of the rusty wood stove. But this weekend Eddie was alone, writing papers for school. Mira was away at her mother's funeral on Long Island.

Eddie was adorably handsome with soulful brown eyes, dark curly hair, and a gentle, playful disposition. He had often stopped by to chat and joke around when I was working at the cleaners, and I found myself watching for the sight of the tall dark figure in the green army jacket coming down the street. Sometimes he brought me a bag of brownies or éclairs from the bakery. His visits and our affectionate banter warmed me through and through. Now, at his cabin, the three of us gathered wood outside and soon a fire was blazing in the rusty stove. Eddie pulled off his hiking boots and army jacket and climbed up to the loft bed where he sprawled lazily, watching David prepare curried rice on the ancient gas range. At dusk, snow began to fall, draping the hillsides in white. Eddie invited us to join him on the bed to watch.

It began so lightly and simply—the falling snow, a warm fire, a close embrace among friends. The embrace led to caresses, and then to kisses and then to deeper kisses.

"Wait a minute! What are we doing?" I said suddenly, pulling back. "If we keep up like this, we'll all end up making love."

"It's okay, Pamie", said David, his hand on my waist. "We're all good friends."

"It feels so right," said Eddie, his soft brown eyes gazing into mine.

Everything was aboveboard, they insisted, unbelievably open and non-possessive—nothing hidden or shameful. So in the warm loft bed with the snow falling outside, we floated away on a river of love.

Eddie claimed later that David and I were planning all along to have sex with him, but he had dropped mescaline earlier that day, so he was probably delusional. As much as I liked him, a love affair—especially among the three of us—had never crossed my mind.

For the next week the three of us carried on our affair and made plans to move together to a big house in the country with Mira, as soon as she came back. But lying in bed at night between David and Eddie, I didn't see how that was going to work. For one thing, the bed was too crowded. Three adults don't fit comfortably in a double bed, much less four. The fact that it was a loft bed with low ceilings made me feel even more claustrophobic.

But the real problem was that I had fallen for Eddie and longed to be alone with him, to explore the sensuous new world unfolding between us. Eddie and I did steal a few hours alone in the cabin one afternoon. I had shaved my legs, unbraided my hair so it fell softly over my shoulders, and put on a long calico dress for the occasion. The pipes in the cabin were frozen and Eddie melted snow for a bath in a little tin tub, pouring water over me in front of the glowing stove. Afterwards, there were hours of tender lovemaking. Dusk fell, snowflakes tapped against the windowpane and logs shifted in the wood stove. The fire went out and the cabin grew chilly, but I was warm in Eddie's arms, his curly head cradled in the crook of my arm. This was paradise—not a revolutionary Eden, but a soulful dark-haired boy.

The week we spent with Eddie was a deliciously impossible tightrope walk teetering on despair. What would happen when Mira came back? I wondered.

"I hope she will find it in her love to forgive me," Eddie said, when I asked him about it.

Forgive him? What was he talking about? Remorse was not part of the revolutionary utopia of love, light, and non-possessiveness.

Mira eventually did come back, but she did not find it in her love to forgive him. The four of us holed up in their tiny cabin in a kind of nightmarish group therapy marathon. Eddie cried, Mira raged.

"How could you do something so stupid?" she screamed.

"We all just kind of—fell in bed," said Eddie.

"You fell into *that* bed?" yelled Mira, pointing to the high loft with its rustic wooden ladder.

David, who had been feeling left out lately, was hoping for a foursome, but Mira refused to have anything to do with us. When she tried to leave the cabin, Eddie stood out in the snow in his bare feet, trying to stop her.

"Fuck you, you've blown it, Eddie, God damn it, let me go!" She pulled Eddie's hair until he cried.

"But Mira, can't you open up and accept what's happening?" Eddie's eyes were pleading. "I love you, but I love Pamie and David, too."

It must have been a nightmare for Mira, just back from her mother's funeral. But all I could think about was Eddie. I was furious with myself for falling in love with him. It was so reactionary of me. At the same time, I was desperately afraid of losing the tenderness blossoming between us, especially when Mira gave him an ultimatum.

"It's either me, or Pamie and David. You decide."

The next morning Eddie walked into the dry cleaners carrying a backpack and some fishing gear and announced that he was throwing his fortunes in with David and me. Later, in the middle of the night, he had second thoughts and walked eight miles over the mountain to Mira. At dawn, he had third thoughts and hitchhiked back again. My moods went from wild ecstasy to hollow despair; his vacillations were tearing me apart.

From the telephone booth outside the bus terminal, I had long conversations with Debbie. She said all kinds of wildly improbable things—we were in the vanguard of the sexual revolution; we were daring to challenge traditional relationships and sexual stereotypes; we were waging a guerilla war against monogamy. I could always count on Debbie to put a positive spin on whatever mess I happened to find myself in, although she herself would never have been part of a ménage à trois.

I wanted to believe what she said, but every cell in my unliberated body longed intensely to be alone with the soulful, dark-eyed Eddie. I sensed that Eddie felt the same way, but he hadn't made an open avowal of love. (In spite of being a revolutionary, I still thought of romance in nineteenth-century terms.)

"I'm thinking of running away to the north woods," I told him. We were sitting alone in the back of the cleaners after hours. Outside, under the street lamp, students hurried down snowy side streets bent forward against the wind.

Eddie held my hand, playing with my gold wedding ring, tugging it back and forth on my finger. "Please don't go. I can't make it without you. I was thinking of going to California, but I don't want to go alone."

If, at that moment, I had said that I'd leave David and go with him, would Eddie have gone? But I never said it, and he never asked.

In the end, Mira extricated him with a knock on our door in the dead of night. She had summoned Eddie's sister and her husband from Maine to help deal with the crisis. Now they were sitting in their car outside our house, their motor running in the dark. I crept out of bed where David lay sleeping, no longer interested in a revolutionary love affair that had forced him out. I sat down at the top of the stairs, shivering as a blast of cold air blew in through the front door where Eddie stood in his long underwear, arguing with Mira.

All through that endless night, Eddie went back and forth between the car and the house, trying to make up his mind. Each time he left I would sit stiff with panic, terrified that this was goodbye.

But Eddie never said goodbye. On one of his trips to the car, he simply didn't come back. Morning dawned, gray and empty. I stared out, hollow-eyed, hollow-souled. How I could go on without him? My lips, my eyes, my hands, my heart—all of me belonged to Eddie. Looking out at the bleak winter landscape, I imagined all the winters of my life stretched out ahead of me, barren of hope or passion.

January came. The snow grew deeper. It covered the rocks and ridges, filled the crevices and coated the shining white cliffs behind our house where, beneath the cold bedrock of the mountain, I buried my broken heart.

There's a Peanut in My Ear!

That spring our landlady rented the main part of the house (attached to our annex) to a group of pseudo-revolutionaries who roared in on motorcycles, accompanied by a pack of snarling dogs, and guns they fired into the furniture at night, tearing our country serenity to shreds. In search of peace and quiet (I never wanted to be a *noisy* revolutionary) David and I moved over the mountain to a small farmhouse on a dirt road winding through a rippling fold of the mountains. At night, we could hear the Coxing Kill stream rushing through the valley, swollen with melted snow.

Our house on Clove Valley Road had a claw foot bathtub with a view of the mountain, a woodstove in the kitchen, and a ghost in the downstairs bedroom that floated out after dark, making the air feel cold and clammy. Our landlord claimed the ghost came from a vanished mountain village on a neighboring ridge, but more likely it was the spirit of the old woman who had died in the house the winter before.

With summer, came house guests, including my mother, who chased the ghost out of the downstairs bedroom. I guess it recognized someone with scarier energy than itself.

Most days, we hitchhiked twelve miles over the mountain to New Paltz and back, lugging groceries and laundry on our backs. I was still working at the dry cleaners and David had a summer job as a gardener at Mohonk Mountain House, a rambling Victorian hotel that stood majestically on the crest of the mountain like a Bavarian castle with flags fluttering from its turrets and towers. Behind the hotel, perched on crags and cliffs, thatched-roofed pagodas looked far out over our house on Clove Valley Road and the peaks of the Catskills rising in the distance.

Like me, David saw himself as a character in his own story, an internal narrative that gave his life meaning and lifted it above the ordinary. From his perspective, Mohonk was a feudal estate with serfs tilling the land to fatten the pockets of the rich overlords. The only reason he put up with it was so he could organize a peasant uprising and overthrow the pigs—i.e., the Smiley family who owned the hotel and 8,000 acres of surrounding wilderness.

It was 1971, the height of the women's movement, and all our misery and frustration, everything that was wrong with our relationship and our lives, we saw in political terms.

We aren't getting along.
Translation: Marriage is a repressive institution.
I feel suffocated in the relationship.
Translation: Marriage is a repressive institution.
I am furious with David for criticizing my writing.
Translation: Men are pigs.

November came, that time when the world fades to gray and sounds fade to silence. Up at Mohonk, walking the old carriage roads that connected the patchwork of forests, fields, and farms, I contemplated my dying marriage and disappointed artistic longings.

At twenty-four, I was trapped in a web of conflicts and contradictions. David and I were comrades in revolution but combatants in marriage; I was a modern woman warrior who spent her days sewing long calico dresses. I longed for an unchanging past even as we plotted to sweep away the old order.

An Incredible Talent for Existing

The fame of revolutionaries like George Jackson, a Black Panther who had recently been killed during an attempted prison break, reached mythological dimensions, but Clove Road remained serene; the only gunshots were from an occasional hunter. David had not managed to organize a peasant revolt at Mohonk, and not a single runaway revolutionary had taken refuge at our house, which was supposed to be a stop on the new underground railroad. We didn't even have the drama of David's going to jail to look forward to. His trial had come up and his lawyer got him off on a technicality.

All this was a strain on our marriage. I decided to go to Brooklyn for a week to stay with George and Betsy, friends and fellow radicals from The New School. There, I would get liberated from male patriarchies and sexual stereotypes.

But sleep eluded me in their small, cramped apartment. I missed David, our country house, and the sound of the stream flowing through the pines. Panic escalated as I lay awake listening to sirens wail, and wondering what was to become of my marriage and the rest of my life. Desperate for peace and silence, I went looking for something to plug up my ears. All I could find was a jar of dry-roasted peanuts in the kitchen.

This will work, I thought, popping a peanut into my ear. Unexpectedly, the peanut broke in two, and half of it slipped down inside my ear. When I tried to dig it out, it went in even deeper.

I knocked timidly on George and Betsy's bedroom door.

"George? Betsy?" I whispered. "I've got a peanut stuck in my ear."

Pamela Jane

It seemed like forever before George whispered back groggily, "Pamie, it's two o'clock! We'll talk about it in the morning."

In the morning the peanut was still there. I could feel it pressing against my eardrum.

"How did it get there?" George asked.

That was a tricky question. I didn't want George and Betsy to know that I, a liberated woman, was homesick and frightened, or that I found it hard to sleep in their noisy apartment.

"Well, ah . . I was eating peanuts and I scratched my ear and I guess part of a peanut must have been stuck to my finger and gone down inside."

George looked incredulous. Then he looked in my ear. "I can't see anything. Are you sure you have a peanut in there?"

I nodded, and the three of us headed off by subway for the Brooklyn Ear, Nose and Throat Hospital. I stuck stubbornly to my story all the way there. The more dubious George looked, the more embarrassed I felt, and the more embarrassed I felt, the more fiercely I insisted that the whole thing had been a freak accident born of eating peanuts carelessly at two o'clock in the morning.

"So, let's get this straight," said George. "Are you saying it's just a tiny piece of a peanut in your ear?" We were sitting in the emergency room waiting to see the doctor.

"George, leave her alone," said Betsy.

"I just want to know," said George.

"Pamela?" said the nurse, "you may come in."

I stood up and walked quickly into the examination room. George followed me.

An Incredible Talent for Existing

"Been partying, eh?" the doctor said with a wink, when I told him my story. He took a long skinny metal instrument and dug the peanut out of my ear. George's mouth fell open.

"Betsy, Betsy, it was practically a whole peanut!" he cried, bursting into the waiting room.

Everyone in the emergency room was staring at us.

"George, let's go home," said Betsy.

I went home too. It was dark by the time I got off the bus in New Paltz and hitched a ride over the mountain to where Clove Valley Road snaked off from Route 44/55. I walked the three miles home in the moonlight with the damp, sweet-smelling river flowing beside me. It had been a very liberating trip. I just hoped the Sisterhood, whoever they were, would understand.

Mohonk Mountain House, New Paltz, NY

"The parlors and porches overlooking the lake, quiet pathways and lacy green arbors recalled the luxury and leisure of a past age."

Fanshen

We decided to give up our house on Clove Valley Road and separate for the winter. Somehow, we hoped, by separating, we would become magically transformed, like the peasants in *Fanshen*, a book about Mao Tse-Tung's cultural revolution in China. ("Fanshen" is Chinese for "transformation.") We were confident that our transformation would allow us to be together in a new and revolutionary way that was impossible for us to imagine in our present reactionary state of mind. We would be real revolutionaries taking action, not impotent dreamers writing imaginary novels and organizing imaginary uprisings. There was work to be done, bombs to be built, blood to be spilled. Blood was the currency of revolutionary authenticity. If you couldn't spill it yourself, you could advocate spilling it, or imply that someone else better start.

David arranged to write for a radical newspaper in Poughkeepsie while I made plans to cut sugar cane in Cuba for the Venceremos Brigade, a revolutionary Chicano organization. The idea of being supported by a rigid, almost military structure was comforting. If I were totally exhausted, I wouldn't have the energy to panic. But the Venceremos Brigade rejected me. I was too politically naïve, they said—not tough enough.

Instead, I quit my job at the dry cleaners and joined Debbie and her roommate in their sprawling sunny apartment in the Mission District of San Francisco. The Mission was funky, friendly and down-home, like the loosely-knit community of radicals and ex-Reedies we hung out with.

Pamela Jane

I spent my time at "Connections," an organization that transported people to visit relatives and friends in prison, and took a class to learn how to tune up a car—in case I ever got one and in case it ever broke down, I wouldn't have to depend on pigs (men) to fix it. Afterwards, I walked home through the gray fog, a metal wrench bumping in the back pocket of my overalls. It was a grim existence I had eked out for myself, but there were also good times that brightened the gloom of my radical exile— all night dancing parties, trips down the Pacific Coast Highway, and campfires on the cold wind-swept California beaches. Nat, a fellow radical and preacher's son from Mississippi, was sweet and attentive, almost adoring but I couldn't think about another man. I was waiting for Fanshen. Fanshen was a powerful disinfectant that would kill the germs of capitalism, romance, the desire for private property and personal privacy. Somehow, it would bring me back to David and a country house cradled on the green slopes of the mountain. I still believed in the boy from Connecticut, the white frame house, and the life it promised of security, safety and tradition. Somehow, for me, the image of mutual love and a full family life co-existed with the vision of a revolutionary future in which everything that existed would be destroyed.

One half of me wasn't speaking to the other half.

As my separation from David drew to an end, I searched anxiously for signs of transformation. As far as I could tell, nothing had happened. Was Fanshen so subtle that I'd missed it?

David and I talked on the phone. "I got us summer jobs at Mohonk, and they'll give us the ski lodge to live in."

Fuck Fanshen. I had sprawled on an oil-stained floor in my overalls, staring up at a Volkswagen motor, which was, to date, the most boring thing I had ever done in my life. I had visited my adopted prisoner at Connections, and kept company with real radicals. It was time to go home.

I was flying home, high above the Rocky Mountains when an inner voice spoke to me. Actually, in the beginning, it was more a feeling that would eventually find a voice. And because I refused to listen, it would drive me into the darkest basement of my soul, ram a stake through my heart and force me to choose between madness and sanity.

Part 4

The Voice of Liberation

Flower Girl

In May David took up his old gardening job and his fantasies of organizing a peasant uprising at Mohonk. In truth, he never did anything but castigate himself for his passivity while sharing brown-bagged lunches with the other gardeners on the broad green lawn that sloped down to the rose and herb gardens. This failure to organize in the face of bourgeois luxury and self-indulgence became a source of bitter contention between us. We had failed the revolution and ourselves; more deeply (he implied) I had failed to help transform him and the world in the image of our Fanshen fantasy.

Mohonk, like our parents, represented something solid and conservative, somewhat stuffy. (On my first day of work, my boss sent me home to take off my long dress and put on a dark skirt and white blouse that made me look like an airline stewardess.) To us, the hotel with its massive land holdings and enormous staff was a monstrosity, employer of the displaced and dispossessed, hated protector and parent. It was all that, and it was beautiful, too. The parlors and porches overlooking the lake, quiet pathways, and lacy green arbors recalled the luxury and leisure of a past age, before the world awoke to its twentieth century horrors.

My job was to gather flowers from the cutting gardens and greenhouses and arrange them into bouquets for the guests. Carrying vases of peonies and lilacs, I walked from wing to wing, down long carpeted hallways, past ornately-carved fireplaces. I could imagine a character in a Henry James novel descending the great central staircase to the ballroom, hear the rustling of silk and the sound of laughter from the veranda, where the candles of the chandeliers reflected in the dark waters of the lake.

But beneath the image of nineteenth-century beauty and civility, a malignant dread was growing. When I closed my eyes at night I saw fragrant bouquets of lilac and wisteria—the companions of my days. But in the dawn the flowers melted away, and I bolted awake with a premonition of terror.

I am the Voice of Liberation. You must leave David and live alone forever.

It was clearly an inner voice I heard. Inexplicably, it was turning on me, painting liberation as a bleak, joyless land, barren of hope or happiness. In spite of my inflammatory rhetoric about men and my clashes with David over my writing, I couldn't visualize my life without him. I loved his dark eyes, his graceful muscular body, the way his fingertips caressed me when we lay in each other's arms listening to the rain. Most of all, I loved our common memories that knitted together the past seven years. Life without David was nonexistence—the flame of a candle blown out.

The "Voice" was more than a voice; it was a frightening inner presence that talked like Mao and looked like Mr. Clean. Terrified of its menacing message, I tried to push it down, to make it very small. In retaliation, the Voice became sharp, like a shard of glass lodged painfully in my psyche, an unrelenting and pitiless persecutor.

I argued with the Voice about who was the crazy one. The Voice insisted *it* was the healthy part of me and represented my liberation.

You don't love David anymore. You can't love any man. You must follow me into eternal solitude.

See how crazy that sounds? You sound like a fucking fascist, I screamed inwardly.

You're the one who's trying to make me *sound crazy so you don't have to listen to me!*

Fanshen was a fantasy. All that remained of our marriage and my dreams were a boy and a girl and a white frame house in Connecticut. I was trying desperately to find my way back there, and into our life together, but my panic shut me out. It was like looking at the slick glassy surface of a mirror and not being able to inhabit the living, breathing world it reflected.

I was unable to eat, and I couldn't sleep for more than a few hours. Sometimes I woke up screaming. By day I was paralyzed by panic and trapped in a maze of endless self-questioning. Was I really crazy or only pretending to be? Was there any difference? I thought of my mom. Is this how she felt before her breakdown, when she paced the house, wearing a path in the carpet?

My inner turmoil made it hard to keep up appearances at work, to behave as if I were one normal person instead of two crazy ones. Even if I managed to forget about the Voice momentarily during the day, in sleep the door to the unconscious swung open, and silently, stealthily my tormenter slipped through.

Panic drove me to frantic extremes. I would decide I had to leave David and then change my mind twenty times a day. Sometimes I waited for him to come home so I could hug him and reassure him that everything was going to be all right. I would hear his footstep outside, and my heart would leap. But inevitably, the sight of him would reanimate all my agitation and ambivalence.

"David, try to be patient with me!" I begged.

He did try to be understanding, but my constant vacillation drove him into long, sullen silences.

One day, sitting in a summerhouse at Mohonk high up on the cliffs overlooking Clove Road, I consulted the *I Ching*, an ancient Chinese oracle. My reading said it was time to get out of the chariot and walk. I imagined the ski lodge on the hill as the chariot pitching our possessions from side to side as it lurched recklessly along. But I didn't want to get out and walk. I wanted to stuff all the craziness back inside and stay with David in the light-filled lodge, watch the roses bloom at Mohonk and see the cloud shadows flit across the mountains where the hawk soared high above the clove.

"Just one more summer," David said.

"Just one more summer?" I asked the Voice. But I knew there would be no gift of another summer.

Looking back, why couldn't I have said, "David, it's not working out between us, so let's go our separate ways in the fall." But it's only in retrospect that one can be so coolly rational. At the time everything was too poignant, too terrible, too real. It was easier to go crazy and run away to some desolate place where I would not be tormented by the contrast between inner and outer worlds, which is what I did later that summer when I left David and the excruciating beauty of Mohonk, and headed north by train to a Quaker commune in upstate New York. I couldn't think about why or for how long, or what would come after. The commune was cheap and I hoped the people would be kind to lost souls.

The train followed the Hudson River to Albany, where I got off and took a bus to a small town. From there I hitchhiked to the commune, a small, dark farmhouse built of stones from the surrounding pastures. In the low-ceilinged kitchen, everyone gathered to eat around a rough wooden table. Ever since the crazy Restraining Arms in Portland, I had hated the idea of communal living. What I treasured most was rural solitude. Yet here I was sitting on a long wooden bench eating brown rice and carrots with total strangers. The Voice decreed it so. With the Voice everything was absolute. Freedom. Truth. Fiction. Lies.

Two sisters sat across from me. One had recently separated from her husband. "We are still good friends," she said. "He will be coming soon." Her eyes looked off anxiously as though expecting him to walk in at any moment. A man sitting next to me was drinking clear broth with what looked like bits of grass floating in it. "Ralph believes that food is poison," the other sister explained.

I was among the lost, the tortured, the exiled. Where I belonged.

That night everyone slept on the floor in one of the bedrooms except for Peter and Steve, two gay men who had a room to themselves. *They'll have each other tonight* whispered the Voice. *And you'll be alone.*

In the middle of the night I got up to go to the outhouse, trying not to stumble over bodies in the dark. The Voice laughed softly, shattering the night into glittering splinters. I had to be careful not to cut myself on them as I tiptoed barefoot down the narrow stairs. *This is your new life,* whispered the Voice. *How do you like it?*

The commune reflected my inner landscape much more closely than the harmony and serenity of Mohonk. This was the gray gulag, the prison camp where people slept side by side on the floor with no privacy and no plumbing, a desolate land haunted by fear.

I had fallen out of my story, out of my life, and into hell.

In the morning everyone left to prune apple trees except for a boy called Leo, who stayed behind to cook dinner. While he puttered around the house, I walked into the woods and methodically banged my head against a tree.

Stop putting on an act, sneered the Voice, unmoved.

Revolutionary transformation was a mad dream, but this was madness as I had never dreamed it, without romance or redemption.

When I got back, Leo was sitting on the back porch, peeling carrots. He looked up quizzically.

For a moment I just stood there, looking at him. Then I took a deep breath and reached across the immeasurable expanse to another soul.

"I'm . . . kind of freaked out."

Leo nodded. His dark eyes were full of sympathy. "I figured."

You're the worst kind of scum, pretending to be crazy, snarled the Voice.

An Incredible Talent for Existing

We talked for a long time that day, and Leo told me how he'd come to the commune.

"I woke up in my dorm room at college one day, and everything felt different, unreal," he said. "I couldn't stay in school anymore so I dropped out and came here."

I could understand that, waking up one day and finding yourself in a strange country with no familiar landmarks, an exile from your own life.

During the next few days people drifted in and out of the commune. One of the sisters left, and the other one spotted Ralph, the man who believed food was poison, wolfing down hamburgers at a fast-food joint. Leo and I spent the long quiet days talking. He was only nineteen, slight and dark, with a sweet, gentle masculinity. I felt drawn to him, but I knew I was too crazy to be with a man.

My panic made it almost impossible to stay in one place, or hold a single thought for more than a moment. I had to do something, go somewhere, get away! If I could run fast enough, maybe the panic would take a couple of days to figure out that I wasn't there before it came after me.

I left the Quaker commune after three days, hitching a ride with a trucker on the New York Thruway. It was raining and the windshield wipers slapped in time to Carole King singing about metaphysical contradictions.

I closed my eyes and drifted into an uneasy sleep.

Win, lose, win, lose, droned the windshield wipers enigmatically.

A Place to Call Home

Two days later I was sitting in the Dutchess County Mental Health Clinic in Poughkeepsie, talking to a psychiatrist. David sat silently beside me.

"You are Pamela?" asked the doctor. She wore a sari and had a kind face.

"Yes."

"What's the matter?"

"I feel—"

"For how long?"

"About a month—panicked. I can't eat. And I hear a voice."

It felt strange to say it out loud. It also sounded a little crazy. The doctor was writing in her notebook.

"What is the voice saying?"

"It says I have to follow its commands because it represents my liberation. I can't eat or sleep." I paused. "And I scratched my arm."

The doctor stopped writing and looked up.

"Let me see."

I pulled my sleeve up, revealing an arm gouged by finger nails.

The doctor's expression changed. She snapped her notebook closed and stood up.

"This is an emergency," she said. "Another doctor will see you immediately."

I was disappointed to lose the lady in the sari. The new psychiatrist looked like a zombie with staring eyes and pale skin pulled tight over his face. I repeated what I'd told the other doctor.

"Is it a man's voice or a woman's voice you hear?" he asked.

The Voice growled.

Shut up, I said silently.

Shut up yourself, Baby. What are you doing here? Go on, play like you're crazy!

"It's *my* voice," I said aloud. "I hear it inside."

"Do you think it's trying to tell you something?"

"I don't know."

Liar.

"You are working against yourself when you don't eat," the zombie doctor said. "You give the Voice power then, which is destructive."

I nodded gratefully. Maybe my panic wasn't the result of a political truth I was too cowardly to face. Maybe I was just crazy, like my mom. This thought was almost a relief because it meant I could get better and live with David. Sitting there in the psychiatrist's office, I had one of my old-movie fantasies and imagined myself convalescing in the rectory garden in a wheelchair with a blanket over my knees, tended by my doting husband.

I didn't tell the zombie psychiatrist at Dutchess County Mental Health Clinic any of my history that day. I didn't trust him to understand. He gave me a prescription for Librium, a tranquillizer, and told me to come back. (I never did.)

As we left, I glanced at David. He looked totally pissed. Craziness was a cop-out. I had betrayed the destruction of capitalism, the smashing of the nuclear family, Fanshen.

Madness was *not* a proletarian disease.

When I left Mohonk for the Quaker commune, I lost my flower girl job. David was still working there, but another couple had moved into the ski lodge. So after I got back, we lived in a Volkswagen bug David bought from a wealthy prep school friend for a dollar.

Now that we were bourgeois car owners, David insisted we pick up every hitchhiker we passed. It was our political duty. Inwardly, I wished we could keep our little piece of portable private property to ourselves. But it was a hitchhiker who told us about a cabin on Rock Ridge Farm, rent-free in exchange for taking care of the horses who boarded there.

"Ask to see Carl or Jo Olson," he told us. "Tell them Randy sent you."

Randy's directions took us past our old house on Springtown Road, down a dirt road that opened to a meadow, the low mountain ridge rising beyond. At the edge of a pasture a circle of horse stalls surrounded a modern, dome-shaped barn.

It was a warm Sunday afternoon in late May, and there were people everywhere, working, talking or standing around. Someone pointed out a woman with a long braid swinging down her back, working near the horse stalls.

"That's Jo," he said. "Talk to her."

Jo was walking towards us already, slouched forward and bow-legged, a wire-cutter sticking out of the back pocket of her overalls.

"Hi," she said, shaking my hand. She had a firm, hard grip like a man. I explained why we'd come.

"Know anything about horses?"

"Not really," I said, gazing wistfully across the pasture where a half dozen horses grazed, peacefully flicking their tails. The only horse I'd ever owned was Silver, a white horse-shaped balloon who met a premature end when my brother stuck it with a pin.

"The first guy who took care of them was an asshole," said Jo bluntly. "He didn't know a fucking thing about horses. Astral, the stallion, has been weird ever since." She paused, looking at us. "Can you guys hang around for a while or are you in a hurry?"

No, we weren't in a hurry. We hung around, petting the colts and watching close of day on the farm. It had been a cool, rainy spring and a chorus of peepers rose from the sodden fields.

Carl, Jo's husband, called to her from the barn. "Honey, I'm going to take Emilia up to the house to start dinner." Emilia was their four year-old daughter.

"I'll be right up, babe," Jo called back. "I'm just trying to get this fucking wire out of the mud."

Their voices sounded warm and relaxed in the spring dusk. I envied them their easy rapport, free of frightening voices and forces. Such freedom was unimaginable to me. The only life I could imagine with David was one in which I made myself very small and very, very still—a mental bonsai garden where pleasures and pains bloomed in miniature. Any sudden movement, even a deep breath, could dislodge an avalanche of panic. I had taken the Librium the psychiatrist prescribed and stopped screaming out loud, but inside I could see a tiny version of myself, screaming my head off.

It was dark when we followed Jo's flashlight up the rocky ridge to their house. As we stumbled along, Jo talked hard and fast about fences and tack rooms and horse stalls, wells to be drilled and roads to be cut. She was still talking an hour later over steaming mugs of peppermint tea.

"There's a lot to do on the farm. We've got to get the fences repaired and put water down by the new horse stalls. I need a new shed down there to store tack and feed in." Jo's gaze shifted to David. "Your husband could help, too."

Jo was a visionary. In her burned an insatiable fire for improvements. And the fuel for this fire was labor to get the work done. She was a doer, not a dreamer like David and me. But a fire burned in me, too, for physical work to ground me, and a place to call home.

"Who knows," Jo was saying, "maybe we can even get water and electricity to your cabin by next fall."

I smiled. She had called it my cabin.

"Talk to the Writing"

The cabin stood in the woods at the edge of the horse pasture, its dark windows reflecting leaves, shadows. It had no electricity or plumbing, not even an outhouse. We had to shit in the woods and lug water jugs from the main farmhouse where Carl's brother, Paul, lived, a quarter mile away. But the silence and seclusion were luxurious.

Inside, the cabin reeked of empty wine bottles, dog hair, and melted candle wax left behind by the last tenants. I thought about Snow White, and the farm wives in George Eliot's novels. They managed perfectly well without electricity or running water. So I rolled up my sleeves and got to work polishing the windows and the blackened bowls of the kerosene lamps.

For some mysterious reason, my mother decided I was finally settled and sent me a box of keepsakes, including Victoria, a beautiful ballerina doll sent to me by a favorite aunt when I was eight. We carried our things to the cabin, David balancing the battered Lucky Charms carton filled with my writing on his head.

That carton looks so vulnerable, I thought, as we tramped barefoot across the muddy fields in the fading spring light.

David was morose about failing to mobilize the serfs at Mohonk. Instead he'd become a serf himself, toiling on the land by day and drowning his sorrows in a bottle of Gallo wine at night. We rarely talked about politics anymore. Our shattered dream of a revolutionary utopia was a bitter reminder of personal and political failures. And David was angry about the botched guerilla war we'd waged against monogamy, with Eddie. Although the subject of Eddie, too, was off-limits,

"I don't mind that you fell in love with Eddie," he said, "what I mind is that you fell *out* of love with me."

"I can't love two men at the time same," I retorted. "I'm not that liberated."

David was right, though; I had fallen out of love with him when I fell for Eddie.

Evenings at the cabin were spent in tense silence. While I sewed, using an old treadle sewing machine and flatirons heated on the woodstove, David downed a bottle of wine or a six pack. Only once did he break his silence.

"I don't want to live a life of quiet desperation!" he burst out.

"Neither do I." (I preferred a life of noisy desperation.)

What appeared at first to be an opening was actually a closing. David never again spoke of his disappointments or regrets.

That spring I got a letter from Robert, a prisoner I had visited at San Quentin as part of an "Adopt a Prisoner" project I participated in while staying with Debbie in San Francisco. He was out of prison, he wrote, and starting a new life in San Diego. I was happy that he was free and away from the fear that had haunted him in San Quentin. I was the one in jail now, in a prison I couldn't escape—my crazy mind.

I remembered how, as a little girl, if I didn't go to school one day, if I had a doctor's appointment or for some reason I was outside the usual schedule, I'd feel the jaws of emptiness yawning, waiting to swallow me up. Though I hated school there was something reassuring about being part of a firmly woven social structure.

Rising alone in the cabin after David had left for work, I felt a gray, beckoning netherworld waiting to envelop me—a way station between here and nowhere, like a hospital waiting room or a bus depot.

I can't go on like this, I'd think. I'll check into a mental institution. Then I'd remember the horses.

I'll feed the horses first, I decided. Then I'll check into a mental institution.

I slipped on my mud-stained overalls and rubber boots and sloshed through the wet pasture to the horse stalls. The horses whinnied when they saw me, anxious for food and freedom. I stroked them as they plunged their noses greedily into their grain buckets, snorting when they got to the little packet of worm medicine. The rain had continued into early summer, and the roof in the barn was leaking. I broke open bail after bail of rotting hay, looking for a sound one. The physical work, and the pungent smell of hay and horses acted as an anti-anxiety tonic. Earth. Life. Reality. The horses pulled me through the first hour. After that it was time to take a bath at the farm house. Then I called Helen at Vick's Cleaners from the pay phone in the tack room. So my day went.

Wake up.

Panic.

Feed the horses.

Take a bath.

Call Helen.

Hitchhike to town (David took the car to Mohonk).

At the cleaners, Helen would make tea, comb and braid my long tangled hair and tell me funny stories to cheer me up.

"You're my angel," she would say, because I'd brought her lunch and cups of steaming tea when she was in bed with a bad back. But with my muddy overalls, crazy inner Voice, and crippling panic, I felt about as far away from an angel as you can get.

After visiting Helen, I'd think about checking into the mental institution, but by now it was time to feed the horses again.

Moment-by-moment, day-by-day, the horses kept me alive with their demands, the simple demand of the living to live.

I've always wanted to be the kind of person who is confident and authoritative even about ambivalence. But that spring, my sense of self, of who I was and where I was going, was as thin as a shadow. Often I was Jo's shadow, following her around while she ran errands on the farm or in nearby Rosendale. Many times I was on the verge of confiding to her, "Jo, I'm in trouble," but she talked so fast about digging wells and building barns that I couldn't get a word in. And I knew that as soon as I told her I was going crazy everything would change. By saying the words out loud, I would be giving them an authentic life, making them true. I changed my mind every two minutes anyway. Possibilities spun past like numbers on a roulette wheel. I'll stay with David. I'll leave. I'll take a bath. I'll kill myself. I'll bake brownies. If I kept quiet, the wheel might stop at baking brownies and no one except David would ever know the truth.

You look back down the years at yourself in trouble and think how easy it would be to get out. But it's just as easy to slip deeper in. I couldn't go on the way I was, but I couldn't imagine a life without David either. All options seemed equally terrifying and impossible. If I could have cut myself in two, I gladly would have given one half to David, to share his fate and his future—if only it could be the *other* half.

Just when I thought I couldn't stand it another second, a miracle happened. Jo stopped talking and took a breath. In that split second of silence, I plunged in.

"I'm about to go crazy and check into a mental institution!" I blurted out.

At first I wasn't sure she heard me. We were sitting in the Rosendale Diner having coffee and she went right on talking. But as we were leaving she mentioned that her husband, Carl, who taught molecular biology at a local college, might be able to help me.

"Carl is a repressed psychologist," she explained. "He loves helping people and he knows a lot about the brain."

And so Carl and Jo rolled cheap therapy into their package deal of free rent in return for the care of nine temperamental horses.

For years, all I had written were secret journals that swelled with rage against the capitalist pigs, the ruling class, and academia. Now, during our weekly talks in the cabin, Carl encouraged me to "talk to the writing."

If it is real," he said, "it will talk back."

I didn't understand what he meant, but it resonated with my sense that everything was alive and everything had a story to tell, even my craziness.

There is something serene about a house with no bowels, no refrigerator humming, no furnace growling, no toilets flushing. It just is. In this "is-ness," with David away at Mohonk, I began to write down what I heard the Voice saying to me. The act of writing broke its stranglehold over me and lightened its dark predictions. I discovered I had not one but many voices clamoring in my head. I called these voices spirits and endowed them with names and personalities. I was a child again, playing with characters, narratives, fictions. There was nothing political about any of this. It was purely, luxuriously personal.

"Breathless shadows move in the evening of my soul." I had written those words when I was sixteen. I had no idea what they meant at the time, but now they described Iris, a gentle spirit, moving through the murky depths of consciousness, throwing beams of light into the shadows like the kerosene lamps in the cabin at night.

The spirits, which included Ilis, a sexy man-hating feminist, and Orchard, a little girl, were as territorial as the horses. Their name for me was Eartha. The original Voice became Ignor, the Voice I had tried to ignore. I discovered he had a wistful side and felt misunderstood. I had demonized my demon.

"You always have the purest motives, Iris," Ignor complained, "and then you leave me all the dirty work."

If I was talking to the writing, the writing was definitely talking back.

"Will I live alone for the rest of my life, or will I get back together with David?" I asked the spirits (on paper). They responded in chorus.

"We can't answer every question,

"Life is more than introspection!"

The spirits gave texture to the long days of solitude and articulated consciousness into fanciful shapes. I wrote playlets about them and became more interested in their interactions with one another than in myself. I was beginning, in the crudest sense, to write stories. Gradually, as I began to relax, the silence and solitude of the cabin grew rounder and friendlier, a benign rather than a threatening presence.

Only Espatch, the spirit of external catastrophe, remained silent.

Revolutionary Crimes

The cabin evolved into a lovely space of soft colors and shifting shadows; the old-fashioned treadle sewing machine stood by the window where the afternoon sun slanted through the fir tree.

Fall came, that time when the ripening fields begin to unravel around the edges like a carpet of red and gold. On warm Indian summer days I saddled Jim, the gentle gelding, and rode across the stream, up the hill through the dappled October sunshine to the ridge behind our old house on Springtown Road. How many strange turns the world had taken since that first autumn four years ago.

Though I was beginning to feel better, the thought of living without David still filled me with panic. Of course, we saw all our problems in political terms. After all, we were revolutionaries forging our way through dangerous territory to new, unexplored shores of nontraditional marriage. Since this great wave would take decades to break, it was natural that our own insignificant lives would be smashed in the process.

These grandiose fantasies gave us a feeling of euphoria. But there was the nagging question neither of us wanted to bring up: were we revolutionaries on the frontiers of a brave new world, or just an ordinary couple breaking up? But no, such an idea was *verboten*—a thought-crime! And so we hurled ourselves into us into a series of confused separations. First I'd go stay with friends in New York. A few days later I'd be back with an idea that we needed to discuss political strategy. David and I would fight bitterly and the illusion of revolutionary transformation would collapse. Then the cycle of euphoria, separation and disillusionment would start all over again.

In town the new Carrols hamburgers was causing a big controversy. The town board wanted to make money and encourage development. The hippies wanted to keep the town quaint. Tensions mounted. After someone hurled a rock through a window, the management at Carrols hired a 24-hour security guard to make sure no more damage was done. One night sitting in the cabin with the kerosene lamps flickering and a fire in the wood stove, David hatched a plan to make a fire bomb and blow the place up.

I stopped rocking in the wicker rocking chair. I couldn't believe he was serious.

"What about the night watchman? He'll be killed."

David shrugged. "Someone has to die for the revolution."

I was quiet for a moment, thinking about the night watchman. He was a regular guy, probably, with a wife and kids. Or maybe he was a kid himself, just out of high school. "He was such a nice guy and a such a good track star," I imagined his friends saying. And now he had to be sacrificed to prove we were genuine revolutionaries and not privileged white kids from middle-class suburbia.

"We'll do it late at night," David was saying.

A vision flashed before me of the Women's House of Detention in New York City. I saw myself with crystal clarity, staring out through the bars at Sixth Avenue.

David was watching me, his dark eyes glittering. A cold fist closed around my heart. I couldn't say "yes" but something about the way he was looking at me made me afraid to say "no."

"Come on, Pamie. We'll be comrades, just like old times," his voice was soft, seductive.

"I have to think about it," I said, stalling. But all I could think about was getting out of the cabin and away from the crazy look in his eyes. I suggested we go over to a friend's house and tell him our plan. "If he likes the idea, I'll consider it," I lied.

A short time later we were sitting on the floor of Ernie's apartment in New Paltz, drinking mugs of ginger tea.

"David has a plan to—"

"*Shhh!*" David cut me off. "Not so loud!" His eyes got that crazy look. But only when he looked at me. When he explained his plan to Ernie (who laughed, not taking it seriously) he appeared vague and deflated.

David and I drove home in silence, and the plan to blow up Carrols was never mentioned again. I was relieved for many reasons, not least because I *really* didn't want to move back to New York.

I was growing weary of radical ideology. The sheer weight of our illusions was crushing. It hung around me like a heavy, clanking suit of armor, a clumsy mish-mash of history, fantasy, and wishful thinking.

David wasn't toiling at a dead-end job at Mohonk—he was organizing. *Clank.*

Our disintegrating marriage was in the vanguard of the revolution. *Clank.*

It's not you I hate, it's capitalism and the patriarchal society. *Clank.*

One day I was walking through the pasture to the cabin when suddenly I stopped, sensing that something momentous was about to happen. As I stood there in the tall grass beneath a fiery maple, the whole edifice of our fantasies suddenly collapsed around me in a noisy heap. I actually heard it clattering to the ground. Then I stepped over the whole mess and walked away, ideologically naked, but free.

"From now on," I told David, "I'm not a revolutionary or a radical feminist or a great novelist. I'm just me." In a single moment I had managed to extricate myself from my illusions; if that meant I was crazy, so be it. David was furious with me for defaulting on our political faith, but in a weird way, it felt clean. I needed reality, even a deeply flawed reality.

It was 1972. The spring before, South Vietnamese pilots mistakenly dropped Napalm on Vietnamese civilians. A horrific photograph showed a badly burned child running naked from her decimated village, screaming. The Watergate scandal was escalating, and in Vietnam Jane Fonda was broadcasting anti-war messages over Radio Hanoi.

One afternoon David and I were sitting by the window near the sewing machine, discussing President Nixon.

"Well, even Nixon is only human," I commented, absentmindedly. I was trying to decide if I should use the blue calico for an apron for my mother or a blouse for me.

The next moment there was an explosion and a hail of broken glass. David stood facing me, the bloody fist he'd just smashed through the window raised.

"Traitor!" he screamed, wiping the blood on my face. "You wear the blood of the Vietnamese people!"

I stood there, letting the blood dry on my face, staring dazedly at the broken window and David's fist, which was bleeding profusely. Blood, guilt, horror—what was happening to us?

David's accusation added to my long list of counter-revolutionary crimes—being bourgeois, being white, not building bombs. Even my panic was a counter-revolutionary crime because it was personal. If there had been a real revolution, I'd be lying in a mass grave by now.

We cleaned up the broken glass, the blood, and the frightening evidence of rage spilling over, out of control. Carl repaired the broken window, and bandaged David's hand, which was not cut deeply in spite of all the blood.

"Every couple has moments like this," Carl assured me, as I scrubbed a blood stain on the wooden floor. It was a comforting thought, but I couldn't believe what happened was just an aberration in an otherwise happy marriage. We had somehow crossed a line and there was no going back, no way to close the abyss that had opened up between us.

At Carl's suggestion, I consulted a therapist in town for a "second opinion" about separating from David. I launched into my usual existential angst about the voices and the basement of souls and selves while the therapist sat in a leather swivel chair, looking bored.

"You'll just have to decide if you're more comfortable living with your husband or without him," he said, when I finished. He sounded cranky.

I paid for *that*?

On the other hand, maybe he was right. Maybe that's exactly what it came down to.

"We'll separate the day after Thanksgiving," I said to David that night. I paused and looked at him. "Where will you go?"

David sighed as he polished off his third bottle of beer and reached for another.

"Back home to New Britain. What about you?"

"I'll stay here, in the cabin."

I sat staring at our socks tangled together in the laundry basket, the innocent victims of a terrible crime I was about to commit by separating them. Yet I clung stubbornly to the hope that, alone in the cabin, I might be able to realize my dream of shaping my outpourings into stories.

In town, Vick's cleaning business had gotten so bad that Vick was forced to take a construction job to pay the help. Helen decided to convert part of the cleaners into a thrift shop. Soon Betty was unloading truck loads of junk from her dad's barn. She moved around the cleaners with new authority, setting out cracked plates, broken coffee pots, and old shoes.

"Dad says we're in for another rough winter."

If I was going survive the winter alone in the cabin, I would need a good wood stove, the kind that could burn a log for hours, Carl pointed out.

In happier days, David and I had pored over the *Whole Earth Catalog*, dreaming of just such a stove. They cost $800 or more though, an unimaginable sum for us. As it turned out, the solution was sitting in Betty's barn.

An Incredible Talent for Existing

"Dad says it's the best wood stove ever made. Fifty bucks, including delivery."

Delivery turned out to be Betty, who single-handedly hoisted the 400-pound stove onto her Dad's pickup truck. Then she bumped through the pasture to our cabin where she and David unloaded it.

We had our first fire in the new wood stove on Thanksgiving Eve. I sat curled on the braided rug thinking about how, in years to come, I would tell my grandchildren the story of the winter I spent alone in a cabin with no running water or electricity. It would be a story of survival and endurance. But most of all, it would be a story of triumph.

Thanksgiving

Thanksgiving dawned with the deep hush of a holiday. Everyone on the farm was away visiting friends or family. David and I stoked our new wood stove and went out for our last walk together. We were hiking along a snowy ridge above the farm, when the fire whistle sounded from Rosendale. But it wasn't until we heard the fire engines tearing down the dirt road, sirens screaming, that we started to run, racing through the woods, leaping across the stream, and skimming over the brown skeletal fields. When we reached the pasture, we saw the gate flung open and fire trucks plowing across the field towards our cabin. The horses raced in circles, whinnying as flames leapt into the sky above the trees. Two tremendous explosions shook the earth. David shot ahead. A second later, he came running back.

"The cabin's in flames!" he cried.

Frantic, I tried to push past him, but he stopped me. "It's too late," he said. "Everything is gone."

Sobbing, I threw myself down and beat my fists on the ground.

The flames were so hot that the cabin had literally evaporated. Its cinderblock feet turned to dust. The two propane tanks exploded. Even the glass melted.

The fire had started because David had not installed the stovepipe correctly, eventually causing the roof to burst into flames. If it had caught fire during the night we would not have escaped. I remembered watching David assemble the stovepipe. Why hadn't I realized he didn't know what he was doing?

The fire engines bumped back down the dirt road as the last plumes of smoke faded into the November sky.

"Does the fire change anything between us?" David asked.

"No," I said. "Nothing has changed." I glanced at David hunched over in the autumn chill, his hands in his pockets. "What about you?" I asked. It was his home, too, that had burned.

David shrugged. "I didn't lose anything in the fire. I already lost everything I had."

I called Debbie from the telephone booth at the bus terminal.

"Our cabin burned to the ground," I sobbed. "All my writing is gone!" I was devastated by the loss of our belongings I had lovingly collected over the years. To me each object was a living thing. But it was the writing alone that implied that I was more than I appeared to be, and held the hope of redemption.

"I'll just be a waitress, living in a motel room," I cried, imagining my future.

"You could never be just a waitress living in a motel room," said Debbie staunchly.

Her comment surprised me. Maybe she knew something I didn't.

The next day David went back home to Connecticut. I had no family home to return to, so I accepted Vick's offer to work at the cleaners again and stay rent-free in his "retirement" home, a rustic one-story house tucked away in the woods overlooking the Hudson River. Vick had built the house for Helen but she refused to have anything to do with it.

"Who wants to talk to squirrels all day?" she said. Helen preferred to gossip with the customers who came into the cleaners.

An Incredible Talent for Existing

There were moments after the fire when I felt a manic exuberance, a defiance in the face of the awful finality of fate. Look at what life has thrown at me, and I'm surviving! The defiance was fleeting, and quickly settled into a long, unforgiving winter of loss and despair. I had never felt so alone and desolate as I did in the house by the Hudson that December, listening to mournful foghorns on the river, and crying. How could I go on, make sense of this loss? Somehow I *had* to keep writing, to pick up the tangled threads and weave them into a thing of beauty and meaning. But I was terrified I would never write again, that I would, like Dorothea Brooke in *Middlemarch*, "sink unwept into oblivion."

If that was where I was going, I already had a good head start.

Sitting on the living room floor looking out on the icy Hudson, I opened a new blank journal and began writing.

"*All the objects I've lived among and spoken with are gone—the old lace and cracked china, the wicker chair with its patterns of light and shadow, my mother's wooden chopper worn smooth by the palm of her hand, my calico dresses with their prints of wild-flowers. Each one was a fragment of a lost kingdom that I had been trying to piece together into a story.*"

I paused and gazed out at the icy Hudson. Sleet tapped against the window as if the world were crying with me.

"*Gone, too, is a place of quietness and solitude where time was full and spirits spoke, the dream of spending the winter on my own, carrying water and wood, lighting the lamps at night—and writing.*"

Even the spirits had flown away, scattering like a flock of startled birds.

But I would have given up everything I lost a thousand times over for the battered Lucky Charms box filled with my poems, stories and journals—a record of my thoughts and consciousness, my very being, since I was old enough to put words on paper. With that gone it was as if I had never lived at all.

It was a hunter who discovered the cabin burning on Thanksgiving morning. Shortly afterwards, I dreamed that as the cabin began to burn, a man came in and was overwhelmed by a feeling that something must be saved. He could not ignore the strong feeling and rescued the ballerina doll, Victoria, from the flames. I had her again, whole and unharmed, her dark shiny hair, delicate tutu, and legs that bent at the knees and ankles, like a real ballerina.

"But didn't you know that my writing was also begging to be saved?" I asked the man.

Spring came once again to the Hudson River Valley. The ice melted, the river swelled, and peepers called from the meadows. At night a soft breeze smelling of fresh roots and wet leaves drifted in through the open window. I cut my hair so it waved around my shoulders and exchanged my muddy farm overalls for new clothes that showed off my figure. When I looked in the mirror, a slim, shapely stranger gazed back at me with dark, shining eyes.

I visited Carl and Jo. The light was growing longer, and the spring evenings were busy on the farm like when we had first arrived, a year ago. But I no longer belonged there.

David called me one night to see how I was doing.

"I've decided to move to San Francisco," I told him. "I can stay with Debbie until I find a place of my own."

There was a pause on the other end of the telephone line.

"So far away?"

I thought about the land I loved that gathered and fell like green cloth into tucks and folds. Over many years and many miles, my thoughts had shaped themselves around its curves and contours, making it my own. I knew I would miss it terribly.

"Yes," I said. "It's time to go."

I'm into Beauty Now

By the time I moved to San Francisco, Debbie had been living there for five years, doing photography and working as a legal secretary. I got a job working as a waitress at Zim's, a San Francisco restaurant chain.

"I'm just a waitress with no past, and no evidence to show that I could ever be anything else," I said to Debbie one night as we sat at our favorite coffee shop on 24th Street, drinking cappuccinos.

Debbie waved her hand dismissively. "I told you, you could never be just a waitress with no past," she said.

Once again, I had the feeling she knew something I didn't. Otherwise, how could she be so confident?

I rented a tiny back-yard cottage tucked away in Noe Valley—a hilly San Francisco neighborhood of modest Victorian homes. It was like a little village of its own with a dry cleaners, a bakery, and a streetcar line.

The cottage felt cozily familiar, like I was back in the cabin. A rose trellis twined around the front windows and the luxuriously big bathroom was dominated by an old-fashioned claw foot tub, like the one on Clove Valley Road. It was quiet and secluded. Best of all, it was a place of my own, something I had never had.

On weekday mornings I waited in front of the bakery on Church Street for the streetcar to take me to my new job as assistant to the president of an international plant nursery. It was a mom and pop business, like the dry cleaners in New Paltz, only successful. But I missed New Paltz terribly and hated punching a time clock, when somewhere, faraway, the sun traveled over the mountain and the light shifted in the trees. These things were the true markers of time.

One rainy winter night when I felt especially homesick, I called Helen at the dry cleaners.

"I miss you, Helen."

"I miss you, too, honey."

"What's it doing there right now?" I asked.

"It's dark, and the snow is blowing off the roof in the moonlight."

I closed my eyes and imagined the snow, the moonlight, the mountains.

"I have the box of fabric scraps you left at the cleaners, safe and sound," Helen said, breaking my reverie.

"Someday I'll sew them into a quilt," I said. "A quilt of stories."

I wanted to be a writer more than anything in the world, but now, at twenty-five, I still could not imagine what kind of writer I might be. Sitting on the front steps of my cottage, I scribbled song lyrics, comedy sketches, and short stories, most of which were bad imitations of Katherine Mansfield.

Every day after work I took the cable car over the hill to the Jewish Community Center to swim. In my mind, I negotiated dangerous waters with amazing agility, gliding through alligator-infested swamps, across choppy channels, and down swiftly flowing rivers. As I swam I pondered my future. Would I ever find someone to love, have a child, or realize my dream of becoming a writer?

I acquired an extravagantly expensive therapist who lived in Los Angeles. After paying for plane fare and therapy every month, I had a hundred and fifty dollars left for rent, transportation and food. But I was convinced that Dr. Duvall, a well-known psychiatrist, was the only person who could help me decipher the meaning of life and the secret of happiness.

Before my first visit I called his secretary to find out how to get from the L.A. airport to Dr. Duvall's office in Westwood. There was a transit strike in L.A. and I couldn't afford a cab.

"Oh, you can't get here without a car," she said.

"How far is it?" I asked worriedly. I was really counting on seeing Dr. Duvall.

"About twelve miles."

Twelve miles was exactly the distance over the mountain from our house on Clove Valley Road to New Paltz where I had hitchhiked every day lugging laundry and groceries.

"Oh, that's okay then," I said, relieved. "I'll just walk."

When I arrived at the L.A. Airport, I surveyed the dizzying jungle of freeway overpasses and bridges with dismay. This wasn't exactly Clove Road. Finally, I took a hotel shuttle bus to Dr. Duvall's office. (Eventually, I got to be an expert in navigating around L.A. using hotel shuttle buses.)

Dr. Duvall was an elderly psychiatrist with a flamboyant personality and a quirky sense of humor.

"The National Earthquake Center is predicting a big quake in L.A. today," he told me one afternoon when I was lying on the couch in his Westwood office. Sure enough, a few minutes later the couch started shaking. I peered over the side and caught him kicking it with his foot.

Dr. Duvall's therapy (minus the couch-kicking incident) was based on the work of Wilhelm Reich, whom I had learned about from a New Paltz friend. Reich was an Austrian-born psychiatrist and the pioneer of "body" therapy, in which deeply-held emotions are released from the musculature of the body. I did a lot of breathing, kicking and yelling on the couch in Dr. Duvall's office. He prodded, pinched and poked me until I was sore. The effect was to make my already volatile emotions even more intense. I became a volcano, a one-person storm center. My love affairs were passionate, intense, and mostly short-lived. And I took the breakups hard.

Every time I broke up with someone, I wanted to jump off the Golden Gate Bridge. Instead I called the Suicide Prevention Hotline. I always seemed to get a guy named Phil. Phil felt like family because of my brother, Phil (who was in Africa). But unlike my brother, who often dismissed me as being melodramatic, the suicide-prevention Phil *had* to listen and take me seriously.

What I really needed was to take my own life seriously by making a plan for what I wanted to accomplish. I didn't get that in Reichian therapy, but just making a commitment to myself was a step towards healing. Like the Tin Woodman journeying to the Emerald City in search of a heart, I was on a journey, a quest to find myself and develop my gifts. And when in L.A. staying at the Hollywood Studio Club (a modest-Spanish style hotel where Marilyn Monroe lived when she first came to Hollywood) or scouring thrift stores on Hollywood Boulevard in search of cast-off costumes from my favorite old movies, the quest felt exotic and adventurous, which appealed to my love of stories and tales.

By now my dad had married his girlfriend, and on my visits back East, Pauline tried to talk me into getting a government job and a hysterectomy. She was convinced that the security of a government pension and freedom from my biological destiny would solve my problems and give me a happy life. We had long arguments about having kids that always seemed to take place in the kitchen at 1:00 in the morning. One night was especially intense with Pauline (who was childless by choice) getting more and more worked up as she described her own hysterectomy years before. My father had gone to bed and Pauline, a chain smoker and compulsive cook, was smoking and chopping soup vegetables while we talked.

"The doctor said, Miss Schiopp, should I remove your ovaries, too?"

Pauline's face took on a look of fiendish triumph. "You know what I said?"

I did know because by now I had heard the story a dozen times. But I knew she wanted to tell me. I also knew she couldn't be stopped.

"What?"

Pauline dropped her voice to a reverent whisper. "I said *take it all.*"

By now she was really excited, breathing hard while she waved the kitchen knife in the air. "Would you rather be changing diapers or discussing recombinant DNA?" she cried.

"Ah—well . . . I guess I never thought about it." I had a feeling that if I gave her the wrong answer she was going to take care of the hysterectomy right there on the kitchen table.

Pauline did care about me, but my romantic notions about domestic life drove her crazy. I pictured myself sequestered in an attic room, writing dreamily while the voices of my family floated up from the kitchen below. When I saw the movie *I Remember Mama* in the Castro Theater in San Francisco, I realized that this fantasy came from the TV series I'd loved as a child, which was a spin-off of the movie. Each TV vignette began with Katrin as a grown woman returning in her imagination to her attic room on Steiner Street. From downstairs we hear her mother calling, "Katrin!" We know this is the voice of the past, the voice of memory and imagination.

"Coming, Mama!"

Walking home over the hills after the movie, the lamplights shining through the fog, I remembered how I used to love those TV episodes. I was intrigued by the big Steiner Street house with the stairs leading to Katrin's room, and the idea that everyday life could be shaped into a story. A TV episode could take a space of time and mold it into a tale with a beginning, a middle, and an end, and a dénouement after the last ad. All the material of life was gathered up and used to create a thing of beauty and economy—a story.

In contrast, the San Francisco I knew in the 1970s was a city of bone-aching loneliness, of gray Saturdays at the Laundromat and failed love affairs (all of which seemed to end on a gray Saturday at the Laundromat), of Sunday afternoons in revival theaters watching old Garbo or Astaire and Rogers films, wishing myself into the stories and the sets I knew so intimately that I memorized what time the clocks were set to. I willed myself inside the movies of the 1930s and 40s. Their furniture was my furniture, their clocks, my clocks, their country houses my country houses. I was never that good at reality anyway; movies always seemed much more vivid, beginning with the films my parents took me to when I was a small child. I had been overwhelmed by the luminous images on the screen and the poignancy of the stories—the sad clown in *Limelight*, the ship vanishing under the dark waters of the North Atlantic in *Titanic* (1953) the lady calling for her lost dog in *Come Back, Little Sheba*—night songs, whose melodies would haunt me forever.

Free of David's criticism and my chaotic family, I gradually grew more confident. I began writing more earnestly, often working sixteen or seventeen hours a day on the weekends. Sitting on my porch among pots of fragrant lavender and mint from my landlady's garden, spiral notebook balanced on my knee, pen in hand, I obsessed about writing the way I had once obsessed about sewing. But now, at last, it was language instead of cloth I was shaping into stories. One of my short stories, "The Sad Decline of Fanny Brook," was published by a literary journal. I sent a copy to David who called to congratulate me.

"I wish I could have said you had it in you," he said wistfully.

I was stunned, taken aback by his admission after all the arguments we'd had about my writing.

"What else have you been doing?" David asked.

"I bought some 1940s lingerie in a vintage clothing store in Hollywood."

"Lingerie?" said David. There was a disapproving silence on the other end of the line. "You sure have come a long way from Clove Road."

I thought about my unshaved legs, my unfinished love affair with Eddie, our unrealized revolution.

"I remember Clove Road," I said. "But I'm into beauty now."

San Francisco, 1973

"I'm into beauty now"
Photograph by Deborah Guyol

Burying Myself in Idaho and Coming up as a Potato

There was no simple step-by-step healing in therapy. There was only time, old movies, the love of costumes, my rose-sheltered cottage and the blue and white tea kettle my boyfriend, Jake, gave me that leaked when it poured. There were fifteen-hour writing days, aloneness, and the romance of perfect orgasms. (In Reichian terms, the epitome of emotional health was complete sexual surrender with someone you loved.)

One night I did have the perfect orgasm with Jake, who I adored in spite of the fact that he was a mama's boy and a big baby. (He sent me love notes at work in baby-talk.)

"My mom would kill me if she knew I was sleeping with the boss's secretary!" he told me when we first started going out.

After my perfect orgasm, I lay in his bed thinking, I've done it! I've had the 100% perfect orgasm, just the way Reich described it. Wait until I tell Dr. Duvall!

Lying in Jake's bed, I waited eagerly to see what would happen next. Would all my thinking become rational, all my decisions healthy and sound? Would panic become a thing of the past?

What happened next was that Jake got up, dragged the telephone into his bathroom, shut the door and called his old girlfriend. Enraged, I jumped out of bed, put on my clothes, and left, slamming the door behind me.

This perfect orgasm thing was obviously a little more complicated than it appeared.

Looking back, I see San Francisco as a time of delayed adolescence during a sexually adolescent era. It was also a time of increased seriousness about my writing and the knowledge that I was capable of the hard lonely work of becoming a writer. But I still needed the crutch of ideology, something external and absolute to believe in, whether Reichian therapy or radical politics. I didn't yet have the confidence to stand on my own.

Six years slipped by, years filled with stubbornly high hopes, failed love affairs, and calls to Phil at the Suicide Prevention Hotline. One night I climbed the hill above my cottage and sat hugging my knees and looking out at the Oakland Bay Bridge like a shimmering diamond necklace flung across the dark bay. I loved the windy hillsides of San Francisco, the steep flights of stairs, the hidden gardens. But I was thirty-one, alone, and unpublished except for one story in a literary journal. I'd quit my job at the plant nursery so I could write during the day, and was working the midnight shift at the International House of Pancakes. I gazed up at the night sky. Were the stars over San Francisco aligned for a move? Dr. Duvall was ailing and later that year, he died—one more reason to leave.

During this time I made plans to do many things, most of which were related to old movies, like my mental institution fantasy. I pictured a large, white frame house in the Vermont woods (somehow it was always autumn with brilliant leaves and the aroma of wood smoke in the air), a bedroom with a fireplace and four-poster bed, and a kindly psychiatrist who looked like Claude Rains in *Now Voyager*, which I'd seen recently at the Castro Theater.

Debbie had moved to L.A., where she was going to law school, after managing an almost perfect LSAT score in the casual contemptuous manner that had irritated teachers in high school.

If only I could move back to the country where, once upon a life ago, I had felt so deeply at home. I put a rental deposit on a house in the redwoods near Santa Rosa, then backed out.

"I'm thinking of burying myself in Idaho and coming up as a potato," I wrote Debbie.

My mother, who had moved to Austin, Texas, came to visit me.

"Maybe I should move to San Francisco," she said, as we raced up and down the hills in my VW. "Or maybe you should move to Austin."

I had just been to Austin. It was hot and my mother's apartment had cockroaches. She got up at 3:00 every morning to hunt them down with a flashlight.

Finally, in an impulsive reversal of everything I ever said I wanted, I decided to move to New York to see Dr. Baker, another elderly psychiatrist and a close friend of Dr. Duvall's. None of it made sense. I hated New York. I didn't know anyone there. I didn't have any money or plans. It was the gap between expectation and result—the classic story conflict—and I was about to dive straight into it.

I quit my job at the International House of Pancakes, and gave notice to my landlady. I knew that I would miss San Francisco, its hills and lights, its mists, and elusive beauty. Most of all, I would miss the San Francisco of 1910 I never knew, and walking home after seeing an old movie at the Castro, the lights flickering over the hills like the effervescent image of a dream.

San Francisco, 1980

My Dorothy Parker spoof (I never smoked.)
Photo by Jun Kobashigawa

Part 5

Starlight

Rediscovering Betsy-Tacy

My first job in New York was as a temporary secretary in an office on Riverside Drive. It was December, and the icy wind blasting off the Hudson River cut like a blade through my thin velvet coat from San Francisco. In the beginning, I stayed with old friends of David's out in Long Beach, commuting on the Long Island Railroad to my job in Manhattan. Standing on the train platform on frigid winter mornings, surrounded by somber figures in black woolen coats and Cossack-style hats, I felt as if I had been exiled to some bleak northern country. New York was the basement of cities, hard and walled in, while San Francisco was the attic with its lacy Victorians and gentle hills rising over the bay.

Across town, on East End Avenue, was the office of the famous Reichian, Dr. Baker, who chain-smoked and nodded off during my sessions. His office looked as if it had been frozen in the 1940s (when he originally leased it), especially the old-fashioned black phone, which reminded me of the telephone in *Dial M for Murder*, the one Grace Kelly was talking on when the hired killer crept up from behind and tried to strangle her with a scarf.

Like Dr. Duvall, Dr. Baker was convinced that my mental and emotional health depended on my finding a man. But for once I wasn't looking for one. I'd screwed up badly with men in the past and I needed a vacation. Also, New York felt bigger and scarier than San Francisco and I wasn't sure how to navigate the social scene. You could be dating a serial killer and not even know it until you saw his photo on the cover of *The New York Post*.

I was horribly, relentlessly homesick for San Francisco. Sometimes, sitting at my desk at work, watching the lights flicker on across the river in the twilight, I'd think about the lonely weekend ahead and dial the Castro Theater in San Francisco, just to see what was playing. The tape would announce a Garbo or a Marx Brothers film, and I'd imagine seeing the movie and walking home afterwards over the lamp-lit hills.

My move to New York was reminiscent of my leap to Portland, when I left with a dime in my pocket and no plan for the future. New York is a tough place to be alone, but it's an even tougher place to be broke. I felt like a tightrope walker, barely managing to keep from plunging into unemployment, homelessness, and desolation. I survived by apartment sitting. Lower East Side, Upper West Side, Downtown, Midtown—I bounced from apartment to apartment, and job to job. But as difficult as New York could be, there was a romance and glamor about it, especially the New York of the old movies—the career girl living in a million-dollar penthouse, the up-and-coming fashion designer, the rich boss who falls for his beautiful secretary. The possibilities were dazzling. There was also something exciting about the real potential of New York, the worlds of fashion and publishing.

I hadn't sewn in years, but the edges of my thoughts were always curling into sleeves and sashes and skirts inspired by costumes in the old movies and inflamed by the glittering vistas of Saks or Lord & Taylor—which I thought of as the great cultural centers of New York. I decided to enroll in night school at Fashion Institute of Technology, a gray, prison-like building on West 24th Street.

My new artist's portfolio bulged with shiny pinking shears, pins, and colored chalk. But the work was grueling and the stiff mannequins draped in muslin had little connection to the dazzling creations floating in my head. Late one night, after a long day at work, my German draping teacher eyed the mannequin I was draping for the fourth time.

"Zat pin has no meaning!" she cried, pointing accusingly to a pin I had just stuck in the mannequin.

I took that as a deeply existential statement about my future as a fashion designer, and quit.

I had a new job working for the head of a law firm in Midtown. During my lunch hour, I browsed through Scribner's bookstore on Fifth Avenue, climbing the winding stairway to the second floor to read in the comfortable armchairs. I found myself drawn to the children's section and the books I'd grown up with—the *Oz* books, the magic books by Edward Eager, the *Betsy-Tacy* stories by Maud Hart Lovelace. Finding them was like rediscovering old friends. I remembered the first time I opened a *Betsy-Tacy* book. I was nine at the time, going on ten.

"Going on ten seemed to be exactly the right age for having fun," the author wrote.

Here was an author who saw into my soul!

Pamela Jane

For some reason I had never read the *Betsy-Tacy* high school stories. But now, twenty-four years later, I submerged myself in Betsy's high school world, the one I wished had been mine. Family, friends, heartaches and crushes—it was all so innocent and fun, and the perfect escape from the loneliness of New York. But I couldn't locate the last book in the series, *Betsy's Wedding*. The bookstore said the book was out of stock. The publisher said it was out of print. Finally I found it in the Staten Island branch of the New York Public Library. I immediately called and reserved it. But I couldn't bear to wait for the machinery of the New York Public Library system to grind into motion. I would take the ferry to Staten Island, I decided, and get the book myself.

On a gray, misty Saturday in early February, I made the trip, watching impatiently as the ferry plowed through the cold, choppy waters. Couldn't the engines go any faster? What if someone else took out my *Betsy* book first? What if the Staten Island branch burned down before I got there? When we finally docked, I ran all the way to the library. I didn't open the book until I was on the ferry again, headed back across the bay. Sitting on the hard ferry bench, my face wet with foam, I began reading.

"Almost choked with excitement and joy, Betsy Ray leaned against the railing as the *S.S. Richmond* sailed serenely into New York City's inner harbor. The morning was misty, and since they had passed through the Narrows, she had seen only sky and water—and a gull, now and then . . . "

I looked up at a gull swooping over the gray water. New York of 1980 had vanished. It was 1919, and I was a young woman returning from a long voyage, and anxious for her first glimpse of

New York. I smiled to myself and went on reading. *"My heart is turning home again, and there I long to be . . ."*

Home. Could I find a home in the world by writing for children? Could I use imagination and memory to piece together a story the way I had once used calico and old lace to create dresses? Would it be less scary than trying to compete in the cut-throat world (as I saw it) of adult literature? There was the specter of my father—the epitome of academic excellence, and my cousins on his side of the family who all went to Oxford or Cambridge. One of my cousins, an art editor for the *London Times*, had married an English lord. Who was I to compete in the world of Upper West Side and English intellectual aristocracy?

There is nothing remotely easy about writing successfully for kids. But in my mind, it felt safer.

When I was eight and living in Michigan, my mother and I had taken a trip to New York to bring my baby doll, Rosemary, to a doll hospital for new arms and legs. It must have been the Mayo Clinic of doll hospitals for us to travel so far. We stayed with my father's brother and his wife, my Aunt Ruth (the one who had given me the ballerina doll), in their apartment on Riverside Drive. I was enraptured by the long, book-lined hallways leading to dim, curtained rooms, the air of mystery, and the mystique of my older absent cousins off at Cambridge University. Now, in New York all these years later, I began writing a children's story about the imaginary lives of a family of dolls, called *Rosemary Goes to New York*.

When I was finished, I sent my manuscript to an editor at Houghton Mifflin, who returned it with a long letter.

"The tone is intriguing," she wrote, "it creates a delicate sense of mystery . . . of darker elements beneath the surface of the dreamlike narrative." The trouble was, she wasn't sure it was a children's book. She didn't really know what kind of book it was. Neither did I. But I kept writing children's stories and sending them off to agents and editors.

One afternoon I found a letter in my mailbox from a famous New York agent. By this time, I was living in an apartment on Lexington Avenue with a roommate who had a thing for fluffy blue toilet seat covers and picking up large sweaty men in bars. She complained about the noise of my typewriter tapping late into the night.

Standing in the lobby of the apartment building, I tore open the agent's letter, hoping that this would be my big break so I could move out and get a place of my own.

"Your stories are intriguing," the agent wrote. "But they all have cracks in the middle. The beginnings don't go with the endings."

This pronouncement sounded horribly fatal. My stories were broken and there was nothing I could do to fix them. They had a genetic flaw, as immutable as DNA.

Last Chance, Idaho

In my family, college was viewed primarily as a male prerogative. I wasn't considered "college material," and my father quickly lost interest in sending me. I hated school anyway, and in the Sixties our attitude about academics encouraged me to turn this into a virtue—i.e., I was so brilliant and precocious that I sensed intuitively how irrelevant and elitist formal education was. But underneath my disdain lurked a closet academic. Secretly, I was dying to study all those dead white men we'd claimed to hate so much. Or maybe it was the romance of academia that intrigued me. (I have deep fantasies of Oxford in the twenties, like in *Brideshead Revisited,* though this has more to do with scouts who clean your rooms and serve steaming pots of tea than with academic life.) At any rate, after I dropped out of Fashion Institute of Technology, I applied to New York University. NYU said I made too much money for a scholarship, yet I couldn't afford full-time tuition so instead I took an evening seminar on Reich.

I was still in therapy with Dr. Baker, who was in his eighties and growing frailer by the day. He smoked like crazy and coughed uncontrollably from emphysema. He had dark circles under his eyes and often nodded off during therapy. But he was the most famous Reichian therapist in the world and I doggedly stuck with him. There was no pinching or prodding; he didn't have the strength.

"Am I getting any better?" I'd constantly ask.

"Just breathe," he'd say, and go into an uncontrollable coughing fit. But unlike Dr. Duvall, Dr. Baker encouraged me in my writing.

"You have so much confidence," he said, when I told him about the children's stories I'd sent out. "Maybe this is what you should be doing."

The Reich seminar, which was held on Friday evenings, was led by an older NYU professor, a scholar on Swift, Shakespeare, and classical literature. A big, imposing man with thinning red hair and glasses, Professor Bell was a larger-than-life figure with a brilliant mind and a vibrant, magnetic presence. We were all in awe of him. Though he was formal and professorial in class, I sensed in him a more earthy, sensuous side, and his green eyes behind his glasses were fiery and intense. I found it hard to look directly at him because whenever I did, adoration came pouring out of my eyes like rays of light, a response I felt was inappropriate in a scholarly seminar. You could analyze emotions but you weren't supposed to fall in love in the middle of a discussion on *The Function of the Orgasm.*

Purportedly Professor Bell was divorced, but no one had been able to break through his formal academic façade. Other women in the seminar whispered about how impossible and inaccessible he was.

"No one can get near him," one woman told me. This inspired me to throw myself into a protracted frenzy of unrequited love that lasted for a year and a half, and sustained me through dozens of job and apartment changes. I wrote long letters to Debbie speculating on the mystery of his resistance to my overpowering beauty and sexual allure. Possibly he had a dark secret, like Max de Winter in *Rebecca*. (I was constantly trying to figure out what movie we were in; it gave me the illusion that something was actually happening.) Or maybe he was bitter about women (but he seemed so kind and caring).

Spring came; the air was soft and warm and tulips bloomed in Central Park. Feeling buoyant and full of hope, I bought a transparent silk blouse and a lacy slip at Saks to entice Professor Bell with.

I was having trouble with a seminar paper, and Professor Bell suggested we meet for coffee to talk it over. I met him in front of Penn Station on a balmy May evening. I had just taken the train from Long Beach, Long Island, where I'd been visiting the friends I'd stayed with when I first came to New York. I was wearing white overalls and carrying (yet another) carton of my writing I'd been storing in Long Beach.

Instead of a coffee shop, Professor Bell took me to an Italian restaurant with a piano player and flowers on the table. Overflowing with excitement, I slid into the booth across from him, opened the menu, and panicked. I couldn't afford even an olive in this place! Mortified, I hid my burning face behind the menu. How could I tell him I was broke? It would sound like I thought he'd asked me out on a date! He must have sensed my panic because he told me that the dinner was on him.

I relaxed and settled back to enjoy the indescribable sweetness of being alone with the man I adored, and having his intense gaze fixed firmly on me. It was one of those rare moments when I felt myself seated deeply and securely in the center of my own life. It is still immediate and fresh in my mind—the rough feel of the white starched tablecloth on my fingertips, the spicy scent of carnations on the table, the sparkle of laughter between us as we exchanged childhood stories.

"I ran away on my tricycle in Saint Paul when I was four," he told me. "I got all the way downtown and was heading straight for the bridge over the Mississippi when the police finally caught up with me."

He's very independent, I thought. *He may not want to get tied down.*

John, as he'd asked me to call him, also mentioned that he consulted with Standard Oil, where he taught writing to PhD women engineers.

And he likes women with PhDs. He'll never go for me.

I chattered away about my lack of direction.

"I'm thirty-two years old and I still don't know what I want to do." His eyes smiled at me as if to say, you are perfect, just the way you are.

Afterwards, when the dinner with John was over, I agonized about whether or not we'd had a real date. I drove Debbie crazy with my questions. Do you think it was a real date? Or not? Maybe it wasn't. But what about the flowers and the piano player? And the fact that he said he hadn't had so much fun in a long time? Did he mean "ha-ha" fun, or romantic fun? Would I ever hear from him again? This was a serious question, because shortly after our dinner, John left to go fly fishing out west, while I spent the summer in the hot, airless apartment I was sharing with the roommate who complained about the noise of my typewriter. Every day I came home from my job at the law firm and stuck my key into the battered metal mailbox, hoping for a postcard from

An Incredible Talent for Existing

John—a word or a sign that our dinner meant as much to him as it had to me. But day after hot dreary day passed, and nothing arrived.

It wasn't until the following spring that John asked me out to dinner again. (Unknown to me, he had gotten a protracted flu over the winter and been sick for weeks.) This time I felt sure it was a real date. I had just moved into my own apartment in Tudor City, on the corner of 42nd Street and Second Avenue. It was a tiny studio furnished with only a few cardboard boxes and a lumpy futon on the floor, but it was mine. I had a lease, a doorman, and a bathtub all of my own. When we came back after dinner, we sat on the futon until 2:00 in the morning talking, while I (extremely nervous) kept looking out the window at the moon shining over the East River.

"I thought you'd never stop looking at the moon," John told me later.

But I finally did.

This new love was sweeter than anything I had ever imagined, sweeter even than Eddie. I had not forgotten Eddie, the shining winter forest and warm fires, and the delicious feeling of unbraiding my hair and putting on a long calico dress just for him. In my letters to Debbie from that time, I found a scrap of flowered calico folded between the pages, fresh and unfaded after thirty-five years. I never did see Eddie again, and for many years before I met John, the heartbreak over our aborted affair lay frozen beneath the cold, snowy mountain in New Paltz. But though Eddie may have broken my heart, John transformed it.

John and I were inseparable that spring, spending nights in my tiny apartment and weekends together at his brother's house in Woodstock, New York. When summer came, he took off out west to go trout fishing again. I missed him terribly. Then, late one night, the telephone rang in my apartment. It was John, calling from Last Chance, Idaho. It was so good to hear his strong, warm voice.

"I've been thinking about you," he told me. "I'd like to spend more time with you. In fact"—there was a long pause on the other end of the telephone line—"I want to spend the rest of my life with you."

I was speechless, and so terrified by the directness and immediacy of his declaration—no games, no evasions—that I got a stomach ache that lasted for two years.

Dante's Fourth Circle of Hell

John and I passed many happy weeks together after he returned from Last Chance. But there was one strange thing. I had never seen his apartment. He promised I could as soon as he finished fixing it up. What needed fixing, I wondered? With his immaculately-laundered white shirts, Scottish Tartan ties, and ever-present briefcase, John gave the impression of scholarly solidity and authority. I pictured his apartment with Persian rugs and firelight reflecting in the glassed-in bookcases lining his study. I could hardly wait to see it.

At last the apartment was ready. We met outside an old five-story brick building in Chelsea. It was September and the straggly trees on West 25th Street were beginning to turn a dusty city gold. I followed John up four creaky flights of stairs to the top floor.

John unlocked the heavy front door. "Come on in!"

I took a step forward, then stopped, stunned. The place looked like Dante's fourth circle of hell—the manifestation of a personal nightmare. In the middle of the front room, standing on end, loomed a gigantic metal bed spring next to an empty freezer with its door hanging open. Papers covered every surface and littered the floor, ankle-deep. Books were heaped on chairs and tables, and boxes were piled up to the high ceilings, leaving only a narrow pathway between. I could see a pair of snow shoes sticking out of one box and a metal divining rod out of another. And in the middle of all this chaos, like a blazing sun radiating warmth, energy, and love, was John.

"I really cleaned it up!" he said proudly. "You should have seen it before!"

I stumbled through dazedly, while John, full of tenderness and solicitude, showed off his great-grandfather's cedar chest and the lamp from his grandmother's ranch in Oklahoma.

I can do this, I kept thinking. We'll clean it up, one paper at a time. But after I gave up my Tudor City apartment and moved in with John, he wouldn't let me throw anything out. For months I patiently shuffled through papers and empty envelopes, and took baths looking out at the Empire State Building and trying not to think about the lumpy gray thing under the tub. Then one day I snapped.

"Can't we throw just *one thing* out?" I yelled, scooping up an envelope from the floor. I'd stepped on it a hundred times. It even had John's shoe prints on it.

"Be careful! That's my Velikovsky letter!" cried John, snatching the envelope from my hand. He was referring to the Russian psychiatrist Immanuel Velikovsky. I had no idea John knew him.

There were many treasures buried beneath the piles of junk, I discovered, such as a rare coin collection and a stunning portrait of John taken by another illustrious friend, the photographer Roman Vishniac.

It became clear to me that I was living with three distinctly different people: the scholarly professor, the earthy fly fisherman who grew up hunting and fishing in Minnesota, and the guy in his underwear lovingly preparing brown rice and steamed vegetables as he walked back and forth across the creaky wooden floors, stepping on his Velikovsky letter and empty paper bags from Red Apple Supermarket. I loved all three of them.

I also loved that John was older, solid—an established and respected academic. I had tried to achieve a grown up life with David, but we seemed more like children playing at life and revolution. The things I had fantasized about—the life of a minister's wife, a cozy church rectory, and children of our own, had all eluded me.

My stepmother, Pauline, later told me she wasn't surprised that I didn't settle down with a man of my own generation because I myself was not wholly of it. She was right—I've always had one foot in the past. I loved hearing John's stories of growing up in Saint Paul in the 1940s—the booming sound of ice cracking on the Mississippi in the spring, the chugging of a steam locomotive pulling a train filled with war supplies up the steep grade between Minneapolis and Saint Paul in the dead of night, his mother ordering groceries over the telephone from Crocus Hill Grocery. His stories vividly recreated the World War II home front in my mind.

Two years after our "date" at the Italian restaurant, we got married at John's brother's house in Woodstock, overlooking the ethereally lovely Ashokan Reservoir, not far from New Paltz. It was August; my brother was off on European explorations, and my parents couldn't come. My mother was dying of lung cancer, and my father had just been diagnosed with Alzheimer's disease. By that time, I had long forgiven him for abandoning me after divorcing my mother. My stepmother, Pauline, had a lot to do with this. When I moved back East she invited me to visit often, opening the way for my dad and me to laugh and reminisce together during the long twilight of his mind.

Though my parents couldn't come to our wedding, Debbie, who had moved to New York to work in a big law firm, arrived with Lucy, a close San Francisco friend. The three of us wore flowing white dresses and wreaths of flowers in our hair. Thirty guests celebrated, including John's two brothers and his ninety-year-old mother.

John was radiant and serene during the festivities, but I was terrified of the seriousness of our commitment after my disastrous past, and of a malevolent voice within that could erupt like a volcano or an earthquake, destroying our newfound happiness. Of course, I can see now that the Voice had been right all along, in spite of its sneering tone and sinister predictions. I *did* have to leave David. But because I couldn't face the truth, I had twisted its message into something menacing and irrational. Still, right or wrong, the storms and conflicts of the past had altered my inner landscape forever, leaving huge cracks that could easily open up again. Who knew what was rumbling under the surface, or what surprises I had in store for myself?

I tried not to think about this as the champagne flowed at our wedding. John, who loved to cook, proudly served turkey, ham and a whole trout, and everyone sang and danced late into the night. The festivities lasted all weekend with people sleeping outside in sleeping bags, under the stars.

Starlight

Several years after John and I married, Dr. Baker died. By then I felt I had submitted to rigid ideologies for too long. It was time to give up orthodoxies and think for myself. I did find therapists—wilderness guides—to accompany me into the interior. I think of them as manifestations of the benevolent spirits who befriended me at the cabin on the farm —Ellen, goddess of self-esteem; Jodie, goddess of empathy; Mags, goddess of meaning; and Kate, goddess of common sense.

The voices are still part of me, but they are more benign now, especially when I put them to work as characters in my books. (As long as they're employed they're relatively harmless, but give them leisure time and they can do real damage.) I've been given various diagnoses for my mental problems, and they're fun to play with but I don't take them too seriously. Except for my panic. I produce weapons-grade panic, and I've never found any medication that helps. My brain just isn't made like other people's. Our lawyer once suggested that John and I leave our brains to a medical university because, she said, "they don't get much of a chance to look at normal brains." But the only way I'm leaving my brain to science is with a note that says "Find something to fix this."

In 1983, after John and I got married, I took a class at The New School on writing for children. I was awed by the other students, who talked casually about their editors at Farrar Straus or Little, Brown. "My editor says . . . " "my editor thinks I should . . . " These were *real* writers with *real* editors.

Pamela Jane

I was having trouble writing a story that flowed smoothly from beginning to end. According to my teacher, my latest story had a crack in it the size of the Grand Canyon. I was determined to learn to plot, something I had dismissed earlier as being too mechanical. During my lunch hours at the law firm, I visited the Donnell Children's Library and checked out dozens of books. The floor of the little room John fixed up for me was covered with stacks of books, sorted by theme, word length, and age level. I analyzed, evaluated, and eviscerated them to discover what made them work, and to prove to all the Mr. Mortems in the world that I could write.

One afternoon, while sitting around a medical lab during a six-hour glucose tolerance test for low blood sugar, I got a new idea for a children's book. Buried in a leather recliner, glugging down countless cups of disgustingly sweet syrup, I scribbled the first draft of *Noelle of the Nutcracker*, a Christmas story about a little girl and an ambitious ballerina doll. When my writing teacher at The New School read the story she said, "If you want to get published, don't write fantasy, don't write seasonal material, and for heaven's sake, don't write about dolls!" She advised me instead to write about my authentic childhood experience.

One of the things I love most about John is his genuine capacity to nurture. But when I complained to him about what my teacher had said about my story, he responded with a remark so outrageous that I grabbed the nearest object (which happened to be a hideous green vase someone had given us as a wedding gift) and hurled it against the wall, where it smashed into a thousand satisfying pieces.

What he said was, "Do you think she might be right?"

An Incredible Talent for Existing

The truth was, my story about an ambitious ballerina doll *was* my authentic childhood experience. As I little girl, I had been impressed by the dedication and discipline of Victoria, the exquisite ballerina doll my Aunt Ruth had sent me from New York. I would put her in "first position" before I left for school and she would still be there, in perfect form, when I came home. But as I peered into her sweet face, it seemed to me that Victoria wasn't happy being a little girl's toy. She longed to be a real ballerina.

Since my writing teacher had told me that no knowledgeable, experienced editor would ever publish my story, I decided to send *Noelle of the Nutcracker* to an obscure regional publisher that might not know seasonal doll fantasies were unmarketable. But Debbie disagreed.

"Send it to a major publisher before you decide no one else wants it," she said in her most authoritative voice. It was fall again, and we were walking down West End Avenue, near her new apartment.

Debbie has a way of saying things that makes you feel it's impossible to contradict her. She once told me it was okay to throw your gum out on the sidewalk. She said it with so much authority and conviction, that for years I believed that there was a special gum picker-upper who came out late at night to unglue wads of gum from the sidewalk.

This time, though, I was convinced that Debbie was wrong.

"I can't send it to a major publisher," I said. "It's a seasonal fantasy about a doll. No one will buy it."

"I think you should try anyway."

Debbie obviously had no understanding of the publishing market. Just to prove it, I queried the editor at Houghton Mifflin who had written me the letter about *Rosemary Goes to New York*. I didn't even try to make my doll story sound interesting.

"It's a Christmas fantasy about a little girl and a ballet doll," I stated flatly. The editor who had liked *Rosemary* had left by this time, but a new editor responded quickly. "Please send your story right away."

I sent it off and waited. Winter came. Every night after work I walked home past the fabric and notions stores on West 39th Street. Workers called back and forth as they unloaded bolts of cloth from their trucks, shopkeepers stood in the doorways, people hurried by lighted windows glittering with jeweled buttons and beaded chiffons. *Noelle* takes place in New York, and I had written a scene in which Ilyana and her mother go to the garment district to buy fabric for her costume in the Christmas play:

Snow filled the air, and a sharp wind whipped Ilyana's woolen scarf across her face as they hurried along past the bright windows of the trimming stores, looming out of the dusk like glittering ships laden with treasures—colored glass buttons and beads, ropes of silver and gold, and fine French laces the color of whipping cream.

Once again I was playing with buttons and lace, but this time I was writing rather than sewing with them.

Six months went by and I didn't hear from the publisher. Finally I worked up the nerve to call. My heart was pounding as I asked for the editor by name, and waited for her to pick up.

"I'm so glad you called!" the editor said, when she answered. She sounded friendly and excited. "We were just getting ready to offer you a contract."

I drew my breath in sharply. Nothing in my experience had prepared me for this moment. I was like the cartoon character who hurls himself at a closed door that opens unexpectedly at the last minute, sending him flying through. All my life I'd heard "No." No, you're not smart; no, you can't write. No, you can't *have written* this story (my eighth grade teacher, Mr. Mortem). Suddenly I was hearing "yes!" I was practically speechless.

"What about revisions?" I managed to croak. I knew from my class that the editor would expect a major rewrite.

"I don't want to change a single word, although the copy editor thinks there's too much starlight." The editor paused.

"You know," she said after a moment, "I don't think there can ever be too much starlight."

John's and my wedding day, August 1983

Part 6

Celestial Fire

Hidden Lake Farm

I was obsessed with escaping John's nightmarish apartment and the lumpy gray thing under the bathtub, which turned out to be a sweater left behind by the old lady who had lived—and died—in the apartment years earlier, before John moved in. On weekends, John and I drove up to Westchester County and fantasized about buying a house and moving out of the city. On one trip, John pointed out a stately white frame house that looked slightly down-at-the-heels.

"This looks modest," he said.

By 1945 standards, maybe. But this was 1985. John was living in a serious time warp. There was nothing modest in Westchester, not even an outhouse. Furthermore, we were broke. John is a brilliant teacher, but he's clueless about finances. He looks at his balance in the ATM machine and thinks that's how much he has in the bank, no matter what checks are still outstanding. Also, when I met John, he was deeply embroiled in a nightmarish IRS mess; his con-man brother had tricked him into hiding his own (Clarence's) funds. The seven-year paper trail leading up to a $250,000 assessment against John was hidden under all those papers on the floor of his apartment, as I was to discover

Pamela Jane

later. John didn't want to hire a lawyer; he was worried he would antagonize his brother. It would take three years, $18,000 in legal fees, and many knock-down-drag-out fights to dig him out.

Meanwhile, our apartment went co-op and we managed to scrape together $3,000 for a down-payment. Our plan was to lease out the apartment and use the extra money to rent a small house in the country. Maybe, if we could put it all together, I could quit my job at the law firm to write full-time.

It was a glittering fantasy, like a brilliant Christmas-tree ornament hanging from the highest bough, but just out of reach because I couldn't believe anyone would actually want to live in our apartment, much less pay for it.

"It's a great apartment," John said. "Look at all the space—eight hundred square feet!"

So I left it up to him to "sell" our apartment over the telephone to prospective tenants.

"It's got a lot of space and the floors are refinished," he'd say, with absolute conviction. "And it has a bathtub and flush toilet off the kitchen."

"What do you mean, it has a flush toilet?" I asked when he hung up. "What other kind of toilet is there?"

John ignored me, and continued to extol the amazing novelty of a flush toilet. We rented the apartment immediately.

Moving out of New York was one of those decisions that intrigue you in hindsight, a turning point when you take one fork in the road and leave the other behind. I could have stayed in New York and gone to NYU tuition-free, now that John and I were married. Maybe I would have become a psychologist or an English professor. We could have owned a New York apartment, a cabin in the Shawangunk mountains, and two retirement funds. But back then unrealized dreams tugged at me persistently—a house in the country and the writing life. So we rented an old farmhouse on a working farm and moved to Bucks County, Pennsylvania, ninety miles from New York. John commuted to NYU three days a week to teach.

Our farmhouse was a square unpretentious structure of white-painted brick. We furnished it with an old family settee John unearthed from his apartment, a battered desk from NYU and a free TV that had sand in it from riding in the back of someone's pick-up truck. Miraculously, most of John's other things—hunting and fishing equipment, canning equipment, photography equipment, rare books that needed rebinding and old shoes that needed resoling—fit into the basement, and we squeezed the rest into the little attic. I bought a white wooden table and chairs for the blue dining room with the deep-silled windows. John liked to sit outside at the picnic table under the crabapple tree and gaze out over the fields where a church steeple rose up from the fold of green hills beyond the pond.

"It's deliverance," he said, happy to be free of his Dantesque apartment.

With my book advance for *Noelle*, I bought a washing machine and dryer for the old country basement. It was magical to be able to transform something as ethereal as dreams and memories into two pieces of sturdy, practical machinery.

We moved to Hidden Lake Farm in early summer when the fields were filled with the fragrance of mint and wild roses. The view from my writing room could have been a page torn from my favorite poetry book from childhood, *Honey for Tea* by Patience Strong:

> *Swing High*
> *Swing low,*
> *Down to the ground and then up you go.*
> *Catching a glimpse of the old green pond.*
> *The church in the lane and the woods beyond.*

It was my dream of a lost rural past that unfolded outside my window, the inner landscape of my childhood. John and country solitude gave me the freedom and confidence to explore that landscape in a middle-grade novel, which was published several years later. I was writing about eleven year-old Penny Poppen who longed, like I did, to live in the country.

"This is so evocative of New Paltz," said Debbie, when she visited from New York. She was a successful lawyer now, working for an international law firm. We were sitting on the guest bed in my white-curtained writing room, admiring the view from its many windows. She was right about echoes of New Paltz. I had gathered around me pieces reflective of my shattered past—a husband who commuted to an academic job in New York, an old country house, a writing room I actually wrote in. It had taken me many years—a long circuitous route through radical politics, Reichian therapy, mornings writing on my porch in San Francisco, and nights talking to Phil on the Suicide Prevention Hotline. Now at last, I was home.

It wasn't that everything was perfect. Aside from John's IRS drama, I was still scared to trust the relationship, afraid that it was too good to be true. Sometimes I lay in the bathtub at the farmhouse, stiff with panic, terrified that the Voice would erupt to torment me and drive me and John apart. One day John came home from New York and found me sitting on the stairs, crying, like Scarlett O'Hara after Rhett walked out on her. John was stumped. What the heck was I doing sitting on the stairs, crying about nothing?

Many years after we moved to the farm, it finally occurred to me that John wasn't going to get scared off by my spooks or thrown by my panic. Most of the time, he wasn't even paying attention.

"Sweetie, you're playing to an empty house," I told myself as I sat in our blue dining room looking out at the flowering crabapple tree. "John loves you. Why don't you just relax and enjoy the relationship?"

This was some of the best advice I ever got.

Hidden Lake Farm

Publication

One morning in the fall of 1986, I walked down our long dirt driveway, past glowing maple trees to the mailbox, where I pulled out a large brown envelope from my publisher. Standing there, I tore open the envelope, my heart pounding. There it was, my book, a living, palpable thing I could hold in my hands—the child of so much heartbreak, despair, and love. Jan Brett, the illustrator (who was on the verge of becoming an industry of her own) had written me to tell me how much she enjoyed reading the story to her daughter. After the book was done, she let me choose an original illustration to keep.

As I turned the pages, admiring Jan's beautiful illustrations, my mind flashed back to 1965 and the high school hallway where I had stood talking to my chemistry teacher on the last day of school. I hadn't thought about Mr. Welch in all those years, but now I heard his voice as clearly as if I were standing beside him.

"I'm not worried about your chemistry grade, Pamela, because I know that one day I'm going to have your books on my shelf."

I sent the first copy of *Noelle* to Mr. Welch and reminded him of what he had said. He wrote back to tell me that he used my letter and book in his retirement talk. When it was over, twenty years after our conversation in the high school hallway, he went home and put my book on his shelf.

After *Noelle* came out, I called Mr. Arrick, my much-loved creative writing teacher from high school. He remembered me and Susan sitting in the front row, and asked me to call him "George," which made me feel like a seventeen-year-old girl again, shy about a teacher I admired.

We talked for a while, and I asked him if he remembered Mr. Mortem, the eighth-grade teacher who kept my story because he didn't believe I wrote it. The two teachers had taught together in junior high school before Mr. Arrick moved over to the high school.

"Sure, I remember Chuck," he said, in answer to my question. "He got drunk and killed himself years ago."

For a moment I was speechless.

"He *killed* himself? I said finally.

"Yeah, he fell down his basement stairs and broke his neck. He was a closet alcoholic you know."

I couldn't believe it. All those years I'd hated him and worked to get even, and he'd been dead!

My chemistry teacher, Mr. Welch, had given me the incalculable gift of a generous, unearned faith when he predicted that he'd one day have my books on his shelf. Through the years I had carried his words with me like a charm. But Mr. Mortem had given me a no less potent charm—a gritty determination to prove he was wrong.

When Christmas came, I went into New York and saw *Noelle* displayed in the glittering windows of the bookstores on Fifth Avenue I used to haunt on my lunch hours. I never imagined my book would actually be there.

I remembered the dream I'd had after the fire about the hunter who went into the burning cabin and was overwhelmed by a feeling that something was asking to be saved. In my dream, he rescued my ballerina doll, Victoria.

"But didn't you know that my writing was also asking to be saved?" I had asked him. Now I realized that in rescuing Victoria, he was also rescuing my childhood and the doll that would inspire my first published book for children.

He had saved my writing after all.

Impossible Journeys Through the Realms of Time

I had always longed for a child, something that drove my ultra-feminist stepmother crazy during those late nights in the kitchen when she was advising me to get a government job and a hysterectomy, while waving a kitchen knife in the air.

In 1994, we left the little farm house on Hidden Lake Farm and bought a home in the nearby suburbs. Six weeks later our daughter was born. Though I didn't realize it at the time, moving to the suburbs was a philosophical inquiry for me. What would it be like to move back as an adult to a street that resembled the ones I grew up on? What realizations would it bring, what secrets might it unearth? It was a question I regretted asking almost immediately because from the beginning I felt restless and confined in the blue frame house shadowed by tall oaks where we live now. I missed the red maple tree, my intimate confidant and companion for nine years, the fields, and the rhythm of farm work that was woven so snugly into my consciousness that I felt displaced without it.

I'm a restless person. Even now my mind hops from one delectable fantasy-adventure to another. We'll move to Derbyshire, England, where Darcy's Pemberley was filmed for the BBC *Pride and Prejudice*. We'll move to Italy, where the three of us lived for several years on NYU's Florence estate; we'll move to Saint Paul, where John grew up, and live in a big old Minnesota house like Spencer Tracy and Lana Turner in *Cass Timberlane*. But the fanciful hop to the suburbs was a real-life move that was not easy to reverse. Our daughter loved the schools; real estate prices tripled, and John was happy here. So the airy philosophical inquiry became weighed down by logistics that were difficult, if not impossible, to dislodge.

I've always been fascinated by aspects of nineteenth-century design, especially banisters and stairways leading to attics and upstairs rooms like Katrin's room in *I Remember Mama* or Jo's hideaway in *Little Women*. To me, stairways are entrances to the ethereal realm of imagination and memory. It is a feeling Proust describes in *Swann's Way*, when talking about his grandmother, ". . . she would have preferred to take a house that had a gothic dovecot, or some other such piece of antiquity as would have a pleasant effect on the mind, filling it with a nostalgic longing for impossible journeys through the realms of time."

Growing up in Berkley, Michigan, in a neighborhood of small, well-kept yards and streets lined with tidy bungalows, I longed for cul-de-sacs and old-fashioned houses with gables peeking through the treetops. My imagination lingered lovingly on any unusual edifice or piece of architecture, such as a corner lamppost or the latched gate. These were props, jumping-off places to the world of story.

Now, as in Berkley, I was living in a house with no full second floor, only pull-down stairs to a space under the roof. I considered buying one of those little half-stairways they sell at Home Depot and leaning it up against the wall of my writing room, like a prop in a stage play—a glimpse of a staircase leading to a world implied but not seen.

In 2005, after years of complications with the co-op board and other minor real estate nightmares, we sold our apartment in Chelsea. We didn't make a fortune, but we did make enough money to add a two-story office addition onto our house, with a stairway and a banister—that magic portal to the past. My addition is like a little farmhouse all of its own. Through the trees outside my window I catch glimpses of shaded backyards, or an occasional deer or fox who wanders out from the woods behind our house. On the top floor, a glass-paned door opens to a little balcony, an idea inspired by the Victorian rooms at Mohonk.

On summer mornings I sit at my writing desk, listening to the grinding of the garbage truck, the cicadas singing in the trees, and John clattering dishes in the kitchen. Once again the sounds of suburban life are beautiful to me in their commonness and familiarity, as when I was a little girl and the labyrinth of sidewalks, playgrounds, and backyards held the secret language of childhood.

Celestial Fire

Story is an elusive thing, and the search for it at times is perilous. You don't know when you start out on that stony trail if you'll make it back with a tale to tell, or if a fellow traveler will find the remains of your narrative bleached like bones in the sun. Irresistibly, the story draws you on, impelling you to discover what lies beyond the fixed images you've recorded. It's like Antonioni's film *Blow Up*, in which a photographer takes pictures in a park of what appears to be a tryst between a man and a woman. He develops the film unsuspectingly, but then he begins to look closer. Hidden beneath the seemingly innocent images is a darker one—a figure with a gun. The photographer blows up the pictures, larger and larger, and discovers what he actually recorded was a murder. The woman was not flirting with her companion, but leading him on, enticing him in front of a hidden assailant. This is what writing a memoir is like. You go back to the past and discover hidden, sometimes dark, forces in the images you recorded. You blow them up and examine them to see what is really there.

The search for my memoir story took many years (twenty-two to be exact). It was like solving a mathematical problem. In order to find the answer, you have to pose the right question: what is this story really about? Then you have to invent the formula to answer the question, because every memoir forges its own form.

I have a formula for my writing process, too. It goes like this:

agony + (obsession x conflict) + panic + 10,000 drafts - total crap = finished memoir

It's like struggling with those slippery equations that had eluded me in algebra class, but instead of numbers, I'm working with themes, structure, and storyline.

It took not only many years to write my memoir, but many miles as well. During years we lived in Florence, I spent hours roaming the Tuscan hills, agonizing over whether I should be writing for adults or for children. Why couldn't I do just one thing and be unconflicted, like other writers I knew?

It is an indisputable fact of my existence that I have two people inside me who are in constant conflict. They don't acknowledge each other. They don't even return each other's phone calls. Not only do they want different things, but each is horrified by what the other wants. If this were a friendship or a marriage, I would conclude that it wasn't working out.

Sometimes my adult and children's writing collide in unexpected ways. Once I was deeply engrossed in writing a sex scene for my memoir and the phone rang, practically making me jump out of my chair. It was an elementary school librarian calling about my author's visit the next day.

"Hi!" she said. "Mayo or mustard?"

"What?"

"On your sandwich! We're ordering lunch for tomorrow!"

It took me a few minutes to wrap my head around that one.

It may not be a sinister figure waiting in the shadows you discover when you examine the past, but self-knowledge, hidden empathy, buried passion.

Recently, when I was cleaning out the garage, I found an old photograph of John, a self-portrait taken when he was twenty-

An Incredible Talent for Existing

six and studying for his PhD. at Columbia while living in an unheated loft in Soho. In the photograph, he's sitting at his desk, surrounded by piles of books and papers; his glasses are beside him and he gazes intensely into the camera. If only I had known him then! But I was only nine when the picture was taken. As I looked at the photograph, an overwhelming feeling of erotic passion swept over me. I wanted to take the years that stretched between us and bend them together.

How often, in my life with John, had I been horrified by the feeling that it was all a sickening mistake; that we didn't really belong together? What had seemed so terrifying, it struck me now, was the overwhelming power of love, of being swallowed up by stars, scorched by suns, obliterated by planetary explosions.

As I stood looking at that photograph that day in the garage, surrounded by John's hunting and fishing equipment, his metal divining rod and snow shoes, the Vishniac photos, I realized how nearly I had missed knowing what it was to love him completely, without reservation. Finding the photograph dissolved the last traces of icy panic, and lit celestial fires between us that at times feel almost other-worldly, as if we are floating on ether.

A self-portrait of John taken when he was studying for his PhD at Columbia

Epilogue

I hadn't been back to New Paltz since I left in 1972. While working on this book, I decided I wanted to return, to retrace my steps and recover the gaps and missing pieces of the past. Most of all, I wanted to find the girl with the long brown braid hitchhiking over the mountain carrying laundry and groceries on her back, and let her know I had not forgotten her struggles, her silence, or her search for a mother-goddess like George Eliot who would put her life into context. That girl craved context. I wanted to give that to her, to wrap my arms and my memories around her. And I wanted to go alone.

On a warm October afternoon, I returned. Little had changed in the years since I'd left. The bank clock still flashed the minutes of each day, the Wallkill River flowed sluggishly past the cornfields. The old stone library, the Homestead Bar, Manny's Art Supplies—I knew every detail so intimately that I had long forgotten to think of them.

"Nothing momentous happened here," the town seemed to say, in its midday doze. "And whatever did happen is long forgotten."

Thirty-five years ago, New Paltz was my town. I walked the streets, worked in the shops, hitchhiked the roads. In the story I told myself, I was an integral part of the town and its past, not a transient, one of those who came and went and left no mark, not even a grave, upon the land. Now I realized that my consciousness had less weight than a butterfly flitting over the warm autumn fields. There was only the town and the land around it, a land without memories or dreams, without the impression of human hopes or passions. All lay in undisturbed tranquility.

I drove across the bridge to the river flats I used to hurry out to on September afternoons after Betty took over my shift at the cleaners. Where the road divided, I went left up Mountain Rest Road, towards Mohonk.

On top of the mountain, flags still rippled from the towers and turrets of the Mountain House. More than a quarter of a century after David plotted revolution, all was prosperous and busy. Late-blooming roses, not blood, spilled over the gazebos. Gardeners worked planting bulbs, tourists strolled under arbors or glided along the lake in canoes. Trucks rumbled up the mountain, carrying fresh fish and expensive cuts of meats. Inside the hotel, silver vases held bright Japanese lanterns gathered by another flower girl. There were no serfs in revolt, no signs of armed struggle, just the discreet hum of a busy resort on a golden October afternoon.

To sleep again on the mountain, to let my bones melt into rock, to dream, was part of the magic of returning. Walking the remote logging trails with only the sound of my footsteps in my ears, I remembered with unbearable clarity the summer I left my flower girl job. Beauty was not beauty then, nor silence comfort.

Over the next few days, the mountain yielded more of its secrets. I discovered traces of Trapps Hamlet, a nineteenth-century mountain community above our old house on Clove Valley Road. You can still see the golden lilac bushes by the vanished dooryards, the old cellar holes, and remnants of family graveyards. Standing there, I shivered; a wind had come up and the air had turned chill. Maybe this really was where the Clove Road ghost came from.

By a coincidence, I found myself accompanying a friend to Carl and Jo Olson's fortieth anniversary party at Rock Ridge Farm, where my cabin had burned down so long ago. I was apprehensive about going. For one, thing I wasn't sure I'd be welcome. When I left, I had been angry with them about not getting more insurance money for the fire—though in retrospect, the $500 they gave me seemed fair enough. I had also developed a transference crush on Carl (something I never experienced with my elderly psychiatrists) and was furious with him for not reciprocating. I even had a hazy memory of pulling a knife on him in therapy, after the fire. I was listening to way too many Bessie Smith songs that winter on the Hudson.

As I drove down the dirt road to the farm that Saturday night, I could see that much had changed. Jo and Carl had built a center for parties and gatherings; there were lights strung in the trees and a fire blazing in the wood stove inside. To my surprise, Jo recognized me.

"I'm so glad you came!" she said, hugging me warmly.

Carl was more circumspect. "Oh, I remember you!" he said. I thought he looked slightly dismayed, and for a moment I felt awkward and out of place. But suddenly he relaxed and smiled. "It's good to see you."

I breathed a sigh of relief.

People were arriving in waves, laughing, talking, greeting each other after years of absence and separation. There was festive music and tables loaded with roast turkeys, hams, and salads. I made my way through the crowd, looking for someone from the old days I might remember, but the only person I met didn't remember anything except the bars he'd hung out in during the Sixties, and he barely remembered those.

While I was standing in line to get food, a man who looked about my age came up to me.

"Do I know you?"

"I used to live on the farm a long time ago."

"So did I." This wasn't surprising. From what I'd gleaned, dozens of people had come and gone over the years, people like David and me, without homes or families, who were drawn to the sanity and continuity of life on the farm. While I was struggling to stay sane, Carl and Jo had been busy building barns and raising children, and sinking roots deeply into the soil.

"I lived in a cabin that burned down," I explained.

"So did I."

"Mine burned down in 1972." Maybe this would place me in his mind.

"That's when my cabin burned."

This was getting weird.

"My cabin was at the end of the horse pasture in the woods near the railroad tracks." I was starting to feel possessive about my burned-down cabin and the little piece of the past I owned.

"So was mine!" He gave me a look. "Maybe we were married."

I couldn't help laughing. "I think I'd remember." The pot hadn't been *that* strong.

Behind us people were waiting to get food.

"We have to talk!" he called, as I moved down the line.

Later, the man-who-wasn't-my-husband found me sitting by the fire, talking to an old college friend of Jo's. He looked excited, lit from within.

An Incredible Talent for Existing

"I figured it out! We weren't married, but if we had been, the cabin never would have burned!"

The man, who introduced himself as Jack, explained that he lived in the cabin before David and I did, and that he'd left because of his wife's gypsy ways.

"I remember you and your husband. Jo asked if I would mind if you stayed in the cabin for a while. You guys looked really down-and-out, like you needed a place to stay."

I nodded. "We were having a hard time."

Jack was quiet for a moment. "I stored all my photography in the cabin when I left," he said.

I caught my breath. "Oh, my God. I'm so sorry."

Tears filled his eyes, and my heart hurt for this person whose story and loss I had forgotten. We hugged, and I felt something shift inside, like an invisible hand knitting together the empty gaps of the past. For a brief moment we mourned the missed chances, the broken vows, the lost words of the Sixties.

Every so often there is a magical coming together of people that can't be planned or anticipated. There was a spirit of love and acceptance at the party that night, and it rested fleetingly on Jack and me in the dreamlike setting with the lights strung in the trees and a fire flickering in the stove. His gypsy wife was long gone, and David and I were estranged, but Jack and I had forgiven each other.

The next day I packed up and started home. As I headed down the New York Thruway, I glanced back at the mountain. A hawk soared high above the clove and cloud-shadows flitted over the hills. In my mind's eye I saw the girl with the laundry on her back turn and wave. I could let her go now. Her long silence was over. She had found a home and a voice in my story. As I watched, she faded, disappearing into the vanished mountain village of the past.

The Shawangunk Ridge

About the Author

PAMELA JANE is the author of over twenty-five children's books published by Houghton Mifflin, Simon and Schuster, Penguin-Putnam, HarperCollins, and others. Her new picture book, *Little Elfie One* (HarperCollins) is illustrated by *New York Times* best-selling illustrator, Jane Manning. Other books include *Noelle of the Nutcracker* illustrated by Jan Brett, and *Little Goblins Ten* illustrated by Jane Manning. Pamela's book with co-author Deborah Guyol, *Pride and Prejudice and Kitties: A Cat-Lover's Romp Through Jane Austen Classic* was featured in *The Wall Street Journal*, *The Huffington Post*, and BBC America. She is a columnist for womensmemoirs.com, and has published essays and short stories in *The Antigonish Review*, *The Philadelphia Inquirer*, and *Literary Mama*. She is currently at work on a humorous travelogue about living abroad with her family in Florence, Italy.

www.ingramcontent.com/pod-product-compliance
Lightning Source LLC
Chambersburg PA
CBHW021143080526
44588CB00008B/195